In Search of Triumph

By Edgar Farinon

In Search of Triumph.

Author: Edgar Farinon.

Translation to English by Edgar Farinon.

Edition by Professor Prime ltda.

Index

Author's professional information	Pg. 05
Author's contact	Pg. 07
Author's letter	Pg. 08
Acknowledgment	Pg. 10
Notes from readers	Pg. 12
Introduction	Pg. 16
Chapter I - Faith, the Key to Success	Pg. 18
Chapter II - The Future of Each Being Depends on its Own Actions in the Present	Pg. 27
Chapter III - The First Great Responsibility	Pg. 36
Chapter IV - The Great Discovery	Pg. 42
Chapter V - The Purebred Dog	Pg. 50
Chapter VI - The Valuable Diamond	Pg. 78
Chapter VII - The Most Noble Tree Seedling	Pg. 111

Chapter VIII - The Worker Bee	Pg. 140
Chapter IX – The Great Leader	Pg. 159
Epilogue – The Successful Human Being	Pg. 209
Points to ponder	Pg. 226
Bibliography	Pg. 239

Teacher and public speaker Edgar Farinon was:

Network director of the CCAA Institute and responsible for personnel training in the branches, in the areas of methodology, management, marketing, reception and sales.

He participated in several courses taught by Geapo in Rio de Janeiro, Joinville and Curitiba and by the Waldir Lima Group in Rio de Janeiro, Foz do Iguaçu, Cascavel and Florianópolis in the areas of administration, finance and sales.

He worked as a training manager in the training of professionals in the areas of teaching, sales and management for the Outstanding Group in Curitiba where he was also a public speaker and responsible for training advisors and supervisors in the sales area.

He was general manager of the E-Commerce Group, where he was responsible for leading and training teams and for training advisors, consultants, supervisors and managers in the areas of sales, administration and education. Currently he works as a public speaker and teacher in the areas of motivation, mindset, brainstorming, sales, people management and related areas.
He was an Oratory professor at Univille University in Joinville, Brazil.

He is currently developing the formation of a franchisor of Professional courses with an initial sales project in America and Europe, and at the same time is available to give lectures and other training in Brazil and in the world.

He has already rendered services to large companies such as: Banco do Brasil, Besc, Univille, The Church of Jesus Christ of Latter-day Saints, CCAA, SRE and others.

He lived in Brazil, Italy and currently in the United Kingdom and has already visited Ireland, Slovenia, Paraguay and Argentina in an effort to expand his cultural and professional experiences.

02/06/2020

Edgar Farinon

Write to the author

Write to Edgar Farinon or contract lectures and other trainings:

www.edgarfarinon.com
escritoredgarfarinon@gmail.com

Dear Reader

I would like to remind you of a very important fact. When we read a book of romance, fiction or similar we usually read it once and will remember the story for years. When we read a book that aims to bring knowledge, it is necessary to reread it from time to time so it could be understood and memorized to capture its essence.

I have often thought about starting this book and I always ended up postponing it because I had doubts about how to approach the matter.

Indeed, when it comes to personal development, there is an almost infinite range of options for the approach. Many writers have already addressed this subject and certainly in each of those I read I was able to learn something new.

In this book I will talk about human socio-spiritual development, based on my own and others' experiences. All the reports I have tested and I can say they are true and real.

Also excerpts from some holy scriptures have inspired me, because even though this book is not about religion, it is a fact that they are a source of inspiration and wisdom and all material and spiritual success is achieved by using them correctly in our lives as a guiding compass.

Throughout the book, I will quote some passages from the "Bible," "The Book of Mormon," and "Doctrine and Covenants."

Edgar Farinon
Author

Acknowledgment

I am immensely grateful to Gildo Rodrigues de Lima, for the moral support and sincere criticism of the initial text of this book, thus helping to make it even better.

I am also grateful for Nezio da Silva's efforts, for having dedicated so many moments of conversation with me and for criticizing the content covered, thus enriching this work with his experience.

I would never fail to express my gratitude to Dalva Alves for the support and correction of the first Portuguese edition of this book and to Enir A. Farinon for the correction of the third edition.

I am also grateful to all the people mentioned in this book, as they, also, have in one way or another contributed to the success of this book.

I dedicate this book to those who helped me directly or indirectly and to all those who through reading seek to enrich their knowledge and get closer to success. I would especially like to thank my children Janis, Pablo and Angus and my wife Lorecí for their patience in the face of my absence, as many hours were spent in isolation working to make this dream a reality.

I reaffirm here my special love also to my father Ulysses and my mother Lucia, for the education they gave me and to my brothers Enir, Edson and Enivaldo who so often helped me to give wings to my dreams and listened to me talk about them. I also cannot forget my dear granddaughter Emilly who, since she was a child, had advice and suggestions to give me and Enny, who is so affectionate.

Edgar Farinon
Author

Notes from readers

Edgar,

I really liked your book! I learned, too. It was gratifying! When you absorb what you read, there is always a bit of who wrote it and so I was able to admire you even more, if it is possible!

A hug and a kiss to you.

Dalva Alves

I am a lover of good reading and upon winning this book I was delighted with its wonderful content. Right after reading it I decided that I would use all the techniques and teachings of it in my life and I am applying and having greater success in my personal and professional life.

I come from a very poor family and my self-confidence was low. With "In Search of Triumph" I strengthened myself and I'm doing everything with more determination and confidence in the victory. I know these techniques were used by the author to achieve international success.

I recommend reading and rereading it several times, because at each moment of our lives we change the interpretation according to what we need to learn. I'm 56 years old, but I still have a lot of dreams. When reading this book, I realized that I can fulfill my dreams.

Understanding that unlimited power is within us is gratifying, as with this we gain strength to pursue the realization of our dreams, objectives and goals.

This book is a precious gift for those we love, as we will be passing on important knowledge of unveiled secrets for personal and professional fulfillment.

Cleusa Francesquet Gowacki.

I want to express my feelings about the book "In Search of Triumph":
A magnificent book which produces high esteem and courage to the reader. A real super empowering book. Be sure to read its amazing content.

Priest Marcos A. Zonatto

A pleasant read and a bedside book for those who don't accept to live for a little bit. It reflects the great knowledge of the author on the subject, who, in the form of a story, managed to cover several lessons of wisdom with references from various cultures.

An indispensable book for everyone who lives for a constant personal and professional growth!

Congratulations on the excellent work Edgar Farinon.

Alexandre Blank

A great book! It's the kind of book to have beside the bed to read and remember the precious information it contains, especially when discouragement hits us. One of the points that struck me the most was the fact that son of God little god is. We have the power we need within us, it is only necessary to learn how to use it and for that it is necessary to develop some virtues, such as: Patience, ability to listen and love and among others learn to dream and realize the dream. This is a self-help book, both temporally and spiritually.

Waiting for the next book...

Sueliton Gomes

Introduction

For a period of four years, I researched and put into practice the techniques cited in this book and made them the foundation of a successful life.

If we analyze more deeply the great names of humanity, we will discover that they also used them in their lives and that the great winners were and are people who have read and learned a lot from other people's experiences.

I would like to point out that we are immortal beings and our power is unlimited. We just need to learn how to use it.

I will approach human capacity in both material and spiritual progress, telling a story that undoubtedly can happen with you, with me, with each one of us. It talks about the life of a character named Dhay, in a fictional story mixed with eternal truths.

The powers attributed to the main characters are fiction, but all the teachings are real and if applied they will make you a successful human being.

In the course of reading, you will learn techniques of human relations, which will help you to progress and to have full success both material and spiritual. Finally, if you seek wealth, personal and professional fulfillment, happiness, etc., you will learn how to achieve it.

Here you will find the secret of success and you will see that there is nothing complex about it, but you will have to put the techniques mentioned here into practice. You will have to be brave and remove all the fear from inside you. Then you will win!
This book is dedicated to you, who like me, still dare to dream and do not settle, but struggle with determination, to make your dreams come true.

I have tried, throughout this book, to follow a current line of study, so that you learn in a new, different and pleasant way the complex world of the human being in all its physical and psychic manifestations, making you better understand yourself and the others in order to face the competitiveness that now exists in the work market, so that with greater ability you can take advantage of this great challenge.

CHAPTER I

Faith, the Key to Success

September 16, 1964 (8:30 am).

Francisco Beltrão, Paraná, Brazil.

It was a day like any other, but a very special one for a young couple. Ulisses and Lucy had
just become parents for the second time to a beautiful baby boy who they called Dhay.

Five years later.

The son asks:

- Dad, where did we come from?

- You are from here! Your mother and I came from Rio Grande do Sul.

- No, Dad! Before we were born!

- Ah! From mommy's belly ... You ...

- Father, before, really before ...

- ...

Time passed and Dhay was always full of curiosity.

- Mom, when I grow up, I'll be an astronaut.

- Ok son!

- I'm going to the moon like the Americans! Then I will see God there, in heaven!

- Son! God cannot be seen ...

- And are we, His children?

- Yes! Because we are His children He helps when we ask.

- Does He always listen to us?

- Yes son.

- Does washing the wounds in the holy water of the fountain make them heal because he listens to us?

- Yes son! For the one who believes everything is possible.

- Even be an astronaut?

- Yes! Even be an astronaut!

- How do I ask God for help?

- Ask with real intention and the Holy Ghost will testify that you have been heard and decide if you will receive help or not (D&C = Book "Doctrine and Covenants"). But remember, always be honest. If you are unjust, God will walk away from you and will not help you.
- If I ask to fly like a bird, will he make me fly?

- Only if you have no doubt.

- Why?

- Because our Heavenly Father has made us powerful. Through faith, we can do everything.

- That's Cool!

The years passed and Dhay grew up in stature and knowledge.

Dhay studied hard because he knew that **no one can grow without knowledge**.

Specialization is one of the secrets of professional success. If we know all the details of the profession, we can make our business grow and if we don't know we will go bankrupt or we will always continue small.

When someone grows up quickly, many say: "the guy is stealing". Sometimes it is true, but sometimes the guy is specialized in what he does and this is the main secret of his professional success. **Knowing your own business deeply is essential**, Mr. Ulysses explained to his little son Dhay.

Lucy loved telling stories to her children and one day she explained to Dhay that God speaks to men also through dreams.

He was fascinated with biblical stories.

It all seemed like fiction, but he believed it, because how could it be a lie if his mother told that with the water from the fountain on the Calvary Hill, (tourist place in Francisco

Beltrão), God healed the wounds. Dhay used to go there with the inflamed wounds and wash them and the next day only the scars remained.

Of course, the biblical stories his mother told him were true!

Each day, Dhay imagined himself receiving an angel in a dream, talking to Jesus Christ or going to the moon and even dreamed of flying.

One day he had a dream and, in this dream, he was in a known place, but he could not remember where it was. The place was an elevation with a wooden house and there was a party. It was night and suddenly he opened his arms, like a bird spreading his wings and decided to fly home! He said he felt good and that he would like to dream again, but he never had that dream again.

Years later Dhay would come to understand, that dream represented his spiritual and material growth. He would become great among men.

The unknown place represents, that **no matter where we are, we can make progress, just knowing the right way**. The high place, means that **we must be attentive to make the right choices in life**, the mansion, represents simplicity and the party, the pleasure of achievement. This means that something simple can be the key to making a dream come true. Generally, **things are simple, but man**

does not believe in simple things and always finds a way to complicate them, thus moving away from the path of prosperity.

Ulisses told Dhay a true story:
One day a humble man decided to set up a hot dog stand, with a canvas that served as a roof and two bicycle wheels to move it around. It was like a popsicle cart, only bigger and with a roof. He went to Júlio Assis Cavalheiro Avenue (main avenue in Francisco Beltrão), under the flap of a building, so that people could shelter from the rain and sun, he worked even if it was raining torrentially; **another secret to success is we must work hard.**

So, there he was, selling hot dogs day and night. Mr. Ulysses looked at that and thought: He will never sell me a hot dog! There's not even piped water! But the youth did not think like him and started to gather to shelter from the sun during the afternoon and to talk at night. It became a meeting place. They sat on the steps of the building to talk, eat sandwiches and drink sodas...

The young drivers of the city also liked the idea and started to park their cars there, in the wide parking lot of the avenue. It became a place to date and listen to music. So, the sandwich maker's wife came along. Now, sandwiches were also served in cars. It became fashionable. Other hot dog stalls appeared everywhere on the avenue but when the competitors appeared the pioneer in the business had already made good money. He rented a place, small inside, (so the rent was cheap), but with a large free area in front. He turned it into a cafeteria, covered the open area and filled it with tables. He put a big billboard in front of it and continued to serve in the cars and accept that the clients sat on the front wall. He continued service the way that each customer preferred. Today Mr. Ulysses is a client because there is piped water.

He got rich! The competitors arrived late, as the clients preferred the new location because it was cozier, served at the table, in the car, on the wall, on the sidewalk ... Option for all tastes.

This is a beautiful example of how a simple idea became a big business and how to make the right choice.

Let's go back to the dream: "He opened his arms", that is, he looked for a way to grow, he did not settle. "And he flew", meaning he grew spiritually and materially. "And went home", means that he has achieved realization. "It was nice" means that following the inner impulses we will be happy. "I would like to dream again" means that we pass up opportunities and regret it later, so we must be careful in our decisions. "Never dreamed again" (that dream type), means that we have many chances in life, but each chance is unique, it is not repeated. You may disagree but I tell you that you may have a similar chance at a different time, but it's not the same. Once it is missed, it is gone. Imagine a plant in a dry region. It rains just after a long time, the plant is almost dead then it recovers, the second rain comes three months later and the plant is now fully restored. Let's analyze the same situation as follows: It rains after a year, but only in the surrounding area so the plant does not receive the first rain, then the second rain comes and the plant receives it, (it is the second opportunity, which is also often lost by some people), but it is already very weak and the plant will never be the same again, regardless of how many rains fall in the future. **Each chance is unique, don't miss it!**

Dhay, who was fascinated to learn, started to read everything he imagined that could bring him knowledge and found that **not everything we decide to look for at a certain moment, is the best for us.** He put aside the idea of flying to the moon and decided to explore the human mind; A much more complex universe.

He didn't realize it, but it was the Holy Ghost his brother from pre-earth life, blowing in his ears what to do. On this day he discovered the key to success in
James: 1:5-7: "If any of you lack wisdom, let him ask of God, that giveth to all men liberally, and upbraideth not; and it shall be given him.
But let him ask in faith, nothing wavering. For he that wavereth is like a wave of the sea driven with the wind and tossed.
For let not that man think that he shall receive any thing of the Lord.".

From then on Dhay started asking God about everything. Now he was on the right track.

CHAPTER II

The Future of Each Human Being Depends on the Actions of the Present

One day Dhay learned one of the most important lessons! He learned that **everything that will happen, good or bad, in our lives depends exclusively on the actions of the present.**

Dhay was at home with inflamed tonsils, a cold and still with his hand sprained and complained to his father:

- Dad, I don't think it's fair that everything happens at the same time: cold, tonsils, hand sprain. This life is unfair ...

- Who do you attribute all this to? Asked Mr. Ulysses.

- I do not know. I just know I don't deserve it.

- Son! We deserve everything that comes to us through our actions.

- Yes, but I'm not guilty of that. I did nothing to deserve such punishment.

- Son! It is not punishment. **Everything that comes to us serves to make progress.** You are responsible, not guilty. There are no guilty ones in this, but you are really responsible. Let's go back to the past. You were indoors having a cup of hot chocolate and eating a slice of bread, when suddenly it came that heavy summer rain and your body took that thermal shock the moment you decided to take a rain shower. The reaction of heat to cold probably caused you to have a cold and inflammation of the tonsils. If you had asked for permission, this would have been explained to you, thus avoiding these two problems. Regarding your hand; if you hadn't gone to play in the building in construction which is not a place to play, you would not have fallen and sprained your wrist.

- Here comes my father with his lessons again...

- It is true, son! Everything that will happen is a consequence of some action.

- Always?

- Yes. And sometimes it has consequences for others too; but the main person responsible for our future is ourselves.

- Could you explain it better?

- Let's take the example of a nation; with both collective and individual effects. What do you think will happen if all the politicians and the population of a nation are committed to working for the country?

- Without corruption and with all the politicians and people working for it, that would be a prosperous nation.

- Right! Wealth would come in the future and it would not be immediate. In fact, some things happen almost immediately, but it is still future. The next second is future!

- Ok. You're right...

- Take another example. What would happen if our country   to war with other nations?

- Death, suffering, misery would come ...

- That would be a consequence of the action of a leader. So far, we've talked about collective effect, let's individualize. Take the same examples. What would be the consequences for the president who has been at war with other nations?

- Bad. He would be murdered, imprisoned or deposed, but surely everyone would hate him.

- What if he and his team transformed the country into a richer and more prosperous country?

- He would be a hero and that is how he would go down in history.

- I'll tell you a true story. "One day a boy started going out with drugged friends. He was not drugged but as time passed, however, he started using drugs and one day in a police raid, he had been under arrest for carrying cocaine. His penalty! Four years".

- Well...Whoever asks receives!

- Yes. But that was the direct effect. In addition, he contracted AIDS.

- How was that, dad?

- In a fight with an AIDS patient, in prison. He didn't want to fight. The guy started to attack him and he defended himself as he could. One wounded in contact with the other and the virus lodged in his body.
- Dad, it wasn't his fault. He didn't want to fight ...

- Yes, but if he had not been involved with drugs, he would not have been under arrest, he would not have fought with the AIDS patient and consequently he would not have contracted the virus and he could still be alive.

- Really! I hadn't thought of that!

- Most people do not know that **a single action can change a lifetime.**

- Interesting...

- Let me tell you another story.

- Okay.

- One day a young man was invited to work as a wall painter. He accepted. He earned a meager salary. One day his boss took him to paint an English school. He became interested in the language and as soon as possible he started studying English. He was one of the best in the class. One day his teacher offered him a class to teach. He agreed and thus learned the first teaching techniques. Sometime later, he moved to the city of Joinville, Santa Catarina. Once there, he didn't get a job as a painter. He decided to teach English classes. Hurrah! He got a job at a language school! A few years later he set up his own educational establishment. Now I ask you, how did it all start?

- With a proposal to learn to paint.

- Actually, before. It started with the idea of going to the bar to buy a soft drink. There he met his future boss. But let me continue the story. After setting up his own school he traveled to the United States and other countries. All because he decided to go to the bar to buy soda.

- Actually, everything happened by chance.

- I disagree. He could have refused the job or if he accepted, he could not take the English course and could be a lazy student thus not being able to take his first class or still not accept the first class, etc.

- I have to agree again.

- Two important facts have happened. The first was when, by chance, I met a friend who lived in Paraguay. I spoke a few words in Spanish and he answered in the same language. I then asked what he was working on. He replied that he was unemployed. I suggested he teach Spanish classes at a language school. He said he didn't know how to teach. I explained that schools give training courses before the teacher enters the classroom and that knowing how to speak Spanish was enough. His eyes shone! I don't know about this friend's future, but perhaps that meeting with me has assured him a prosperous future, but everything will depend on the decisions he will make.

- And the other fact, what is it?

- It's the story of a discouraged guy. Unfortunately, this is also true. It happened to a friend of mine. He was the typical discouraged one. Whenever I saw him and asked him how he was doing, he said: "Bad, very bad, nothing works". Actually, things were not good for him, but the problem is that he did nothing on his own.

- What do you mean?

- At that time, he had gotten a job as a water filter salesman. He was trying to sell them, however, there was one problem. He used to arrive at the establishments to show his product, with a sad and tired face. It conveyed negativism to people. He was unable to captivate customers and everyone tried to get rid of him soon, perhaps they did it unconsciously. One day he told me that he was going to stop selling filters because he had been trying for a week and he hadn't sold a single one. He stopped it! His boss, a resident from Pato Branco, a neighboring city and coincidentally my friend, that week visited me and talked about the story of the discouraged salesman. I already knew the fact, but I didn't tell him. Then he, a very happy guy, said that he would sell himself in this city, because he did not believe that there could not be a single citizen in the city of Francisco Beltrão who was not in need of a filter. I, who had not bought from my discouraged friend, ended up buying from him, after he happily and showing love for life and people, conveyed a feeling of peace and joy, explained the details of the filter's operation and the advantages of drinking filtered water, in addition to the disadvantages of drinking unfiltered water, etc. Something that the discouraged salesperson, had not even thought to explain to me. He didn't even offer me a filter. Since all this was not enough to convince me to buy it, he gave me a discount. I bought the filter! Well, he had already sold the first one. He left my house and returned three hours later for lunch and had already sold four in a single company he visited; one that the discouraged one had visited and sold none. It is necessary to transmit joy, show friendship and love towards customers. It is also worth remembering something else he did, which is of paramount importance; **spend as many minutes as needed talking about other matters as per customer satisfaction.** On the other hand, **sometimes it is necessary to be brief so as not to take the time that the client does not actually have, in this case it is necessary to approach the subject briefly and very objectively.**

- The teacher commented on this subject. He said that **we should always radiate joy, this is one of the great secrets to captivate people.**

- A couple, after a few years of marriage, saw this one falling apart. I was able to analyze the situation very closely. Whenever the husband sought his wife for affection, she repeated: "Now I can't, let me do the house work" or "Now I'm sleepy and tired", etc. The husband feeling tired of all that got divorced and today he lives happily with another one who gives him affection and values what he does. Contrary to the first, which, however much the husband tried, she found only defects on him.

He of course had his share of blame, but the lack of love was the main reason for the marriage to collapse.

So, son. What do you think of it?

- I do not know... I do not know what to say!

- This is another secret!

- What?

- Listen.

- ...

- When we listen to others, we learn and we make progress.

People who talk a lot usually do not listen and are people with a very limited point of view. Those who get lost in boasting trying to be admired for what they say they have done end up becoming boring and of little value to others and learning very little. Remember: **The greatest sage is the one who listens and is humble to learn from others' experiences.**

CHAPTER III

The First Great Responsibility

Seven years later.

- Mom, I'm so afraid. My first job! I'm afraid I won't do it well!

- Son, never get discouraged. **Everything can be done when you want.**

- I'm afraid of doing something wrong that the boss won't like.

- He knows it's your first job. Don't worry. But I'll give you some tips:

- **Listen to everything and speak only what is necessary and what you feel is useful.** That will bring respect to you. We are judged by what we say and mainly by what we do. When we act and speak in the right way, people start to admire us; but it takes time. **Once respect is earned, we can lose it by a single action or word.**

Consider this example: an employee works his whole life doing his job in the right way and few will value him, but if in a certain situation he makes a serious failure, perhaps in a moment of nervousness he says some rude words to his superior, he may not fire the employee, but perhaps he will never see this employee as a good one anymore. Everything good he did is forgotten and he is now considered a bad employee. Remember that a good deed usually goes unnoticed, but a single mistake may never be overlooked. I remember a curious fact at school. I was always a great student, but one day there was a disagreement and I said some rude words to the coordinator. Today, as you know, I am a renowned businesswoman, but that coordinator who is today the director received me very badly and I lost a deal that my competitor ended up closing, just because I made the mistake of losing my temper just once in my teens, at that school. This coordinator forgot every day, minute after minute of obedience that I gave her during all the years I studied there.

- **The true leader never loses his temper.**

- But mom, leader is leader. Might is right, and obey whoever is sensible.

- Wrong! **The true leader is calm, courteous and disciplined; but firm in his orders.** He gives orders and is always in charge of executing them, but with sensitivity, without rudeness. In this way, the employee feels the duty to obey and respect the "nice boss!"

It is also very **important to follow a schedule** and this applies to everyone regardless of function. If the employee starts to be late, the boss will no longer sympathize with him. This makes it difficult to get a promotion. Try to never be later. However**, if you are late, don't use excuses, tell the real reason for your delay**. The lie is likely to be discovered and the excuses are known to the leaders. See the most usual excuses that any boss knows: Something related to illness, (yours or someone in the family). This is certainly the most used. The car that broke down, the traffic jam, the bus that either passed before or didn't come, etc. It may even be true, but the boss knows it is probably a lie. It would be better to say: "I'm really sorry and I would like to be excused for not having woken up on time," etc. Anyway, speak the truth. The boss will know that the employee was negligent, but at least he was honest and trustworthy. On the other hand, the boss must fulfill his commitments to the employee to set a good example. You should also do your best not to keep other people waiting, as time, whether for a businessman, salesperson or anyone else, is precious and really means money. Consequently, the person who waits feels gratified if attended to immediately, without delay. This certainly makes them appreciate those who attended them, to be a resourceful person, (maybe this happens unconsciously, but it happens). To avoid inconvenience, it is important to record everything from commitments to agreed values, etc.

In case of doubt about what was said related to any operation involved in a conversation it is possible to check what was actually said leaving no room for doubts or discussions.

It is also important to schedule the time for each activity so you can use every minute of your day wisely. When we don't plan, we end up wasting time, doing nothing between one activity and the other, in addition to dedicating time to less important things, making it impossible to remember at any given moment the most important thing we have to do. We must also have common sense to know when to take a break from an activity. Sometimes we are tired of a certain activity and produce less than our potential allows. So, it is prudent to do something else and return to that work later, so we will produce more and not get so stressed is necessary to be sensible, because completed work means free time for something else, however, we always have to be careful to try and complete our projects because leaving many unfinished tasks wears us out psychologically. Be cautious about this. We must also not work harder than our strength allows. For example; a person who does not work on Sundays and does not wear out thinking about business on that day will return to work more mentally rested. Another thing that causes us stress is the fact that when we don't give ourselves time to rest and do other activities our brains end up thinking about work 24 hours a day and this is stressful.

- What do you mean, mom? What about the time we sleep?

- Let's take an example. Suppose I took you to an exhibition of snakes and there by accident, dozens of them escaped and spread around the hall and you were there in the middle without knowing how to get out, terrified to see the snakes approaching you. So, when everything seems lost, you see a window and run away unscathed.

- And...?

- What do you think you will dream when you sleep?

- I will have nightmares with snakes, by the way, I will see snakes even when I close my eyes.

What if on a trip to Rio de Janeiro, you end up dating the most beautiful girl from television?

- I would marry her!

- What would you dream about, guy?

- I would dream of her.

- Okay, what I mean is that we dream about what we do when we're awake. If we don't have time for anything but work. What will we dream about?

- About work, so what?

- The brain accepts the dream as something real. When in a dream, we have no idea that we are dreaming. Worries and mental fatigue happen as if we are awake and working, that is, for the brain we work 24 hours a day.

- Interesting ...

- Some time ago I was on the verge of a nervous breakdown, I felt totally stressed, I didn't know why! I only knew that when I woke up, I was more stressed than the day before. One day I woke up in the middle of a dream and I could remember it: I was behind the desk in the office, with piles of bills and desperate, not knowing what to do. That day I found out that I was working asleep! I changed my attitude. After leaving the office, I refused to think about business. Bring work home on weekends, no way. What happened was that the stress ended and I started to produce much more at work and find solutions to problems more easily.

CHAPTER IV

The Great Discovery!

- Dhay, listen to what I'm going to tell you!

- Who is talking?

- I come from a spiritual world to bring you something that will change your life!

Dhay terrified by that voice, tries to escape, but his members do not respond to his wish.

- Do not be afraid! I'm your friend! I won't hurt you!

- Why don't I see you?

- Because I have the power to hide myself from human eyes.

- Then show up, please, so that I can see you!

- Here I am!

- Well at least you look like people, not green and have no pointed ears!

- Listen carefully to the message I have to give you.

-!?

- All power is within you, just search for it and you will move mountains with thought, if you wish. Everyone can, if knowing how!

-!?

- We are all children of God and we hold the power of the gods within us.

- I do not understand what you say! What gods? What a power?

- We were created in the image and likeness of God and so we have divine power within us. We just have to learn how to use it.

- How can I learn that?

- That's what I came for! I will give you the key to unlimited power. This key has a name, which expresses exactly what it is! Faith!

- Faith?

- By faith we were all created. By faith the world exists and the universe moves and lives in harmony. By faith Moses opened the seas and by faith Jesus Christ healed the sick. Yes. "All things are possible to him that believeth.". (Mark 9:23).

- But, faith in what?

- In Divine power. Do you think I can disappear?

- Yes. I saw you appear, so you must be able to disappear.

- "Because thou hast seen me, thou hast believed: blessed are they that have not seen, and yet have believed."! (John 20:29). So, only then will you have full power, which is all about exploring 100% of your brain.

I'm here to teach you how to conquer unlimited power.

- How do I do that?

- By faith, remember? He who believes everything can! I must go now.

- Wait. I...

That "Enlightened Being" was gone and Dhay was there without understanding what happened. How could he get the faith? How to do everything? And what did "everything" mean?

Dhay thought about starting by moving a glass with the thought. He hesitated. Maybe a feather ... it didn't weigh that much. He stared at the feather and it moved and went to rest gently on the floor, but it was moved by the breeze that blew through the window. He had failed.

Dhay had a wart on his foot. He thought; tomorrow it will be gone. Three hours later he checked to see if it had started to disappear. Ten minutes before the new day, another check. Nothing. He disbelieved. He had failed in faith.

The fact of looking to see if the wart was disappearing, was already a lack of faith.

He called for the being that neither the name he knew and had no answer. He thought, "He won't be back." He failed again in the faith. He insisted for a week. He begged, he humbled himself. He recognized that he had no control over his own life and that he had no power to make the "Enlightened Being" (so he called him) return. All week long just thought about the promise of that being. He called for him and promised to listen to him carefully and do whatever he asked him to do. He recognized himself as a simple mortal who knew nothing about his own life, about the world we live in, much less about a single spiritual world. Nor did he know how to reach this spiritual world, much less how to communicate with the "Enlightened Being". Finally, he understood that we are nothing if compared with this complex universe in which we live in. Because his humility, the "Enlightened Being" returned some weeks later! Dhay had overcome the first barrier: humility!

- You are doing well, keep it up!

- I cannot wait anymore. I can't move even a feather with my thought.

- Patience is one of the attributes of the gods.
The "Enlightened Being" left him, once again. Patience was the next obstacle. This was becoming a game. Dhay was impatient. He failed, but he had learned the humility that would enable him to gain patience.

A few days later, walking around the city, he stopped to listen to a priest of an evangelical church. Surely it was not by chance that he stopped there! Something inside stopped him! There he would learn one more lesson! The priest said:

The Lord knows everything! We have to be patient and wait, as everything must happen in due time! **Impatience and pessimism kill human beings spiritually. Keeping calm keeps us resistant, because nervousness wears us down spiritually and physically.**

It is also necessary to get rid of the old man, to **abandon old foolish habits and traditions. We have to analyze everything and see what is profitable and true. We must also love our fellows as we love ourselves. This will be good to others and bring us many friends.**

- Yes. Dhay had understood. He should be patient, forget old habits, analyze everything, love the others and be persistent. He would wait as long as necessary for the "Enlightened Being" to return!

Six months had passed and nothing. But Dhay was still waiting. He wanted to get that power that the "Enlightened Being" had spoken to him!

Three months later

- Hi, I'm back. Did you forget to call me?

- No. I just thought the best should be to let you decide when would be the best time to come back.

- Wise man! The second obstacle won; the patience. Now we can start the most important part!

- Which is it?

- The wiseness and intelligence! You must seek the most precious treasures on earth!

- What treasures are these?

- For now, you just need to know the first one. You must plant a seed and let it grow a strong plant!
If you acquire the treasures, unlimited power will be given to you as a reward.

- This is hard! Impossible!

- I'll give you the tools to achieve everything.

- And what are they?

- Plant the seed and wait for it to grow a strong plant.

Dhay woke up early and went to the front yard, but suddenly stopped! What seed? And what for? He began to analyze, he had to plant a seed, but he did not know the usefulness, but if the messenger had not said what the utility was, it must be because he would have to decide! He spent the whole day analyzing the situation. He should plant the seed and let it grow but what seed?

Twenty-two days passed and Dhay still hadn't figured out which seed to plant.

One day, passing in front of a plant store, he decided to go in and take a look and find out about the resistance and the time that each one took to grow. He was surprised to learn that some would take his life time to become adult and strong, others less time. Looking at a lime tree, he noticed that a Guanxuma tree grew beside it (Small plant approximately 30 cm high with extremely resistant fibers common in southern Brazil). Yeah! It was the ideal plant, that would grow in a month or two and it was very resistant; it is true that it was not a tree, but the "Enlightened Being" had not said tree, but plant!

On his way back home, he watched over the path to see if he saw a Guanxuma tree with seeds. There was one in a plot of land. Full of black seeds. He chose one that seemed the best and left. He took a pot and filled it with fertilized soil, deposited it inside and watered it with a small amount of water and soon a little plant started to sprout. It grew and grew and three months later it was strong and grown. Mission accomplished. It was worth having patience!

CHAPTER V

The Purebred Dog

And now, what would he do? It was then that the "Enlightened Being" appeared to him and told him that he would have to seek the next treasure: the purebred dog. But how to do it? He needed a purebred race. However, studying dogs, he found that most of them originated from the mix of breeds. After getting a list of purebred names, he said goodbye to his parents and went around the world looking for his dog. He visited many cities in Brazil and in Curitiba he met a bearded and not well-dressed beggar. He stopped. Something attracted him to that man. A beautiful contrast. Dhay in a suit and the beggar all torn but clean.

Said the beggar:

-Your Guanxuma keeps growing. Let it get to the sky and only then will you find your dog!

Startled, he took a step back and ran into a very fragile man with a walking stick. The old man cursed him for bumping into him. Dhay apologized in every way and when he saw that it was no use, he fell silent and just listened to the old man cursing him while watching the curious people laughing at him as he was being humiliated in public: Let it be, he must have a lot of problems to get out of control that way, Dhay thought. And he felt sorry for him.

Then he turned to ask the beggar how he knew about the Guanxuma. Then he realized that the beggar was gone.

He moved on and after a long and exhausting search; two days with no result he went on to Amambai, Mato Grosso do Sul.

He wasn't sure why he went there, he just felt that he should do it and one day later there he was. He found out that there was a man there who used to sell dogs of different breed, all purebred. It was late and he decided to sleep. He had a dream, and in this dream, he was a farmer who was buying Zebu cattle, to set up the largest dairy farm in the world. He woke up and thought: "Yes, I must take the dog from here to Francisco Beltrão!" He turned on his side and slept again. He dreamed the same dream and then a great fear came over him when he was going to sign the check to buy the cattle. He woke up! He couldn't sleep anymore. He knew there was something wrong. But what? He was no longer sure whether or not to take the dog! He thought for the rest of the night and at daybreak, he remembered that Zebu is beef cattle and not dairy. He understood then that his dog was not there.

He slept peacefully, all morning long, and then took a plane to Brasília, the Capital of Brazil. There a policeman approached him, asked for the documents and then gave him an arrest warrant.

- But sir, what did I do?

- Shut up! This is your only right!

At the police station he was subjected to an interrogation about a bank robbery. He denied everything, because he was innocent!

Then, two policemen took him to the bathroom where he was faced with a toilet bowl full of feces. It was there that they put his face several times. But he did not confess to the crime because he had not committed it! He was subjected to a series of electric shocks. They almost killed him. Begging them to stop was no use. He still had nothing to confess.

Then came the drowning. First shower and a superior voice told them to stop. Dhay then, feeling protected, complained about the mistreatment to the superior, who told him to shut up. He claimed his rights and went back to being tortured by being forced under water. They took him out after a few seconds!
- Do you know your rights?

- Yes sir!

- Will you turn to them?

- Yes sir!

- Kill him! And throw him in the lake!

- Wait! I won't complain about anything. Let me go my way.

- Ah! Humble boy! If you open your mouth you die!

- It's ok...

- Take your money and documents and get out of town in twelve hours. Is everything there or something missing?

- Two hundred reais are missing!

- What?

- All right...

- Twelve hours! You want to live, don't you?

Brasilia Airport

- "You must think with your brain and heart"!

Dhay turned, but saw no one and couldn't identify where the voice came from.

- "You must think with your brain and heart"!

Now the voice came from above. He looked but saw no one.

- Got it. The beggar ... the voice ... The "Enlightened Being" guides me!

- What did you say, sir?

Asked a gentleman at his side.

- Nothing. Nothing...

Now he knew without a doubt that he would win!

He went to the ATM to withdraw some money. Balance 0.27 cents! "But how? Impossible. There were over 20 thousand reais there!"

What could Dhay do now? He went to the ticket agency and begged for a ticket to anywhere. Nothing! The clerk threatened to call the police if he continued to insist.

He left the airport and sat on a bench in a nearby square and wept bitterly. Then he remembered! "Think with your brain and heart". He thought... thought... and nothing! He started walking! He walked for miles, until he finally passed in front of a house, where a Rock'n'roll band was practicing! A beautiful sound! But the drums were out of rhythm all the time. He stopped and rang the bell. Some seconds later he was welcomed by a bearded and poorly dressed, but very polite, old man.

- Yes?

- I was passing by and as I am a musician and I liked the music I decided to stop just to say that I liked the music! Sorry if I'm being inconvenient ...

- No. You really aren't! It's good to know that someone likes our sound. What do you play?

- The drums...

- You must have observed that we don't have a drummer ...

- Well...

- My brother tries to play until we find a replacement but as you see, it is not easy for him!

- ...

- Well do you want to play? Let's see what you can do ...

- It's ok.

São Bernardo do Campo - São Paulo.

Two months later.

- As we know, some American band managers and event organizers will be here today. We're just going to open the big band show. We have ten minutes, so let's do our best. Let's try not to make any mistake. If we play well maybe we can be invited to play abroad!

Ten minutes later.

On the stage.

- With you the Brazilian group, "Brazilian Rock"!

The band entered the stage and Pablo the leader introduced the group.

- On the solo guitar; Angus. On the base; Pablo. Bass guitar; Enzo. And on the drums; Dhay.

Ten minutes of sound and the band leaves the scene to make room for the stars of the night.

In the dressing rooms, a businessman is waiting for them to invite them to participate in a benefit show in Salt Lake, Utah, United States of America.

- Brain and heart! That's it! I got a job using the brain. With my heart I will find my way!

- What did you say, Dhay?

- Nothing. I just thought out loud, forget it.

**Salt Lake, Utah,
The United States of America.**

- The show was a success! Don't you think?

- I think so, Angus.

- Shall we go for a walk, Dhay?

- No. I will settle some business in the Temple Square.

- What temple?

- The Mormon Temple. I'll be back in the afternoon.

Dhay then started looking for his valuable dog, not knowing why he was in that city. He just knew he used the brain and got a job. Then he used his heart and put on a show for the benefit of needy people.

- In front of the monumental Mormon Temple, the city's postcard, Dhay said a prayer to Heavenly Father and felt his chest burn with joy.

It was then that someone touched his shoulder and greeted him.

- Hi! Excuse me?

- Yes?

- I loved your show. I'm an organizer of events and would like to hire your band for a tour in the United States. Small places. Cities without much importance. But we will make a lot of money. Here is my card. Call me this afternoon and by the way this Temple is a beauty! No?

- Very beautiful!

- The Lord lives there! See you later...
He plunged into dreams. More shows, more money. Everything would change! He came back from his thoughts with the sound of a voice over his shoulder. It was the Brazilian beggar.

- Small world! No?

- You? How can it be?

- Today you will learn one of life's greatest lessons! Let's sit on that bench.

- Who are you?

- You always have unimportant questions. **Forget everything. Just focus on your goal! Don't forget that fatigue increases if you don't stay calm and focus on** the goal! **Do not work more than your strength allows, but do not be idle!**

- But just thinking about my mission already makes me discouraged!

- **Never worry about the distance you have to go, just focus on the next step. Remember the wise popular saying: look after the pennies and the pounds will look after themselves! Always keep the goal in mind. How to achieve it, God will show you, if you believe.** Then when you look back you will see the distance you have traveled without being overwhelmed!

- Okay...

- You must get your dog in Egypt.

- In Egypt! It's super faraway!

- Less than the distance you have already traveled to get here!

- But I used my brain and heart! Or not?

- Yes! This route is correct. Here you will earn money to spend in Egypt. Save every penny. If you waste a single one, you will fail. **Spend only on useful things. Always invest in what will give you a return!** This requires wisdom! A prophet of God named Brigham Young said something you should never forget: **"If you want to get rich, save what you earn. Any fool can win. But it is necessary to be wise to save and use wisely."** Don't forget Dhay; only the wise win in life. Have you noticed that some poor people become rich, while others live their lives in misery?

- Yes. Why does that happen?

- Most humans are conditioned by the situation they live in. They think about not losing the job they have. For example: instead of studying and professionalizing to get a better and better job, they think about not losing the little they have and forget that they can get much more. Others are **the ones who become rich because they dream and make plans and are never too lazy to fight and are never happy with what they have. They always seek more.** The latter are wise!

The idlers think the wise ones are idiots, because they work hard and are dedicated to growing, as well as making the boss's company grow, (in the case of employees).
The most dedicated will be promoted of course. They do their best for the business they work for. It is these types of people who move the world. They will have chances upon chances to progress, as they create an environment conducive to it!

- Gosh, you are too wise for a beggar!

- Never judge a book by its cover! Remember that work always seems more tiring than it really is. Procrastination disturbs us day after day, year after year. Also remember that most of the time things are not what they seem!

- What do you mean?

- In the future, you will understand, that your dog is not the dog you think. Just as the person who is helpful and friendly can be a traitor! "Wolf in lamb skin"!

Take care of old habits. They limit growth. There was a man who was in the habit of making jokes with people and never stopped it. Yes, he missed the position of supervisor of the company where he worked, because nobody took him seriously. He, however, keeps saying. "I want to die playful".
Being playful is cool. I am also. But there's time for everything! This man, therefore, did not learn the simple principle that everything has its proper time and place.
We should always work on something we like. The work is too exhausting when done unwillingly!

There was a man who worked half his life dissatisfied teaching classes. Always waiting for a chance to change. He forgot, however, that nothing is easy. He only succeeded when his business went bankrupt and had to work as an employee. From there on, he started to have free time. What did not happen when he taught and administered the school. He started to fill his spare time with activities that he liked and at the age of 35 discovered that his gift was to write. Today he is a famous writer and has obviously quit his job. He lives off his books and is very happy. He follows his path with his brain and heart and never forgets his main goal. **The absence of a defined goal is the main enemy of success,** because if we do not have a goal, we walk like an ant that has lost its nest and seeks crumbs here and there repeating the same path, time going north, time going south. He will hardly get anywhere. We have to know what our goal is so we can plan how to get this goal.

- Ok. I got it.

Dhay looked to the side and looking back to where the beggar was, he realized he was gone. However, in the place where the beggar was, there was a book, and on the cover, it was written: "The Search of Triumph - The unlimited power is within you."

He looked at his watch and realized that four hours had passed.
It was time to go and tell his colleagues about the tour. He took the book without imagining that there he would find the secret of his success. He never imagined that from then on he would no longer have the beggar's presence and that that book was a treasure he had in his hands.

Five months later.

- Wow! We are getting rich and we are already kind of famous.

- Yeah. Now that we have been invited to record a CD, we will be famous.

- I need to go to Egypt. You will have to find another drummer. Maybe Rick. He's better than me and he's unemployed since last week when the band broke up.

- What? Egypt? Are you crazy?

- I have a mission to accomplish. Now I need to go.

- You must be kidding!

- No. I have already talked to Rick. If it is ok, he starts today. I will stay until he learns the songs and go.

**Two months later.
Egypt, Cairo.**

- Please sir, is there a pedigree dog seller around here?

- Yes. Your dog is at the end of the street.

- Who are you?

- Dhay. When are you going to learn to ask the right questions?

- Excuse me.

- This is the dog!

- A Pincher? I imagined a big dog.

- **The biggest and most important things go unnoticed in the eyes of men, because they find them insignificant.** Do you see that street and the cars passing by?

- Yes.

- The street and cars are like chances in life. They are not noticed because most of them seem insignificant. That's why we ignore them.

- Are you an "Enlightened Being"?

- Wrong question again. So are men. They are always worried about unimportant things. It is like being in a lake and while the fisherman could have the hook in the water, he keeps cleaning the dirty fingers of the previous fish. Losing the chance to hook the next one.
No, Dhay. I am not an "Enlightened Being". I am a sage who once knew an "Enlightened Being". Now I help others to achieve full wisdom. **If you want to win, focus on the tasks you have to do and forget the unimportant things.**

- It's ok. Thank you very much.

- Now, go to the end of the street on the opposite side of ours and give the dog to a boy who is crying.

- But ...

- Do not argue. Your mission was to find an authentic dog. This is done. He will be yours forever. One day you will understand. Go and make that child happy with this gift. Now I suggest you get the precious diamond.

- Where will I find it?

- Follow your own footprints and when you find it you will know.

- I can't follow in my footprints. They are behind me and not in front!

- Go. I've done my job. Now the rest is up to you!

- Please. Teach me more. Help me.

- It's ok. Go, give the little boy the gift and come back here, then we'll talk.

Dhay hurriedly left. He felt that moment was very important and as soon as he handed the dog over to the boy, he would return to speak with the wise man.

- Wow! Already back?

- Yes. I'm eager to learn.

- Good, very good. This is the attribute of the gods and all successful people have this attribute. This is a very important step. Keep it up and don't forget your book.

- Okay.

- Are you reading it already?

- No.

- **A Book on the shelf serves as much as a fur coat in the summer.**

- I'll read it.

- In addition to reading it, open it whenever you don't know what to do. It will be a guide for you.

- It's ok.

- Something you should never forget is to focus on what you are doing. If you do something thinking about something else, you will not produce as much as you can. It doesn't matter if it is at work, sports, studies or on the mission you are on now. Be aware that the steps of success are invisible. Also **don't waste time, because it doesn't come back. Each second once passed is gone. What is not done in this second may never be done again and if it is, you will have to use the time that would be used for something else.** Wasted time doesn't come back. The time we spend in idleness or doing useless things is lost forever, whether you know it or not. We live an average of seventy years. Infinitely short time compared to eternity. Once wasted, it means part of life thrown away. I suggest that you **have an agenda always at hand with all your daily activities scheduled.** Once this schedule is followed, the day will be better lived. I know that sometimes what we plan can take longer than supposed to. It is then necessary to eliminate something less important from that day's schedule. In other situations, there will be time left, in which case it is necessary to have some activities scheduled apart to fill the empty time. It is also necessary to schedule weekly and monthly and even annual appointments so you will always know what to do next, not wasting the precious time of your life. If we do not schedule our appointments, in idle hours we will think about what to do and we will often forget something of paramount importance and do something less important. We must also be careful not to spend time with things that will not bring us good results or pleasure. The energy spent could have been used in activities that would help us achieve the greater goals of our life and we should never work at an activity that we do not have inspiration to, as we will never be able to do it well and we will not find personal fulfillment. The tendency is that we will increasingly hate it and that will make us unhappy.

- Isn't it possible to get used to what we do and start enjoying it?

- No! If we do something we like, we will not only be happy, but we will fall in love with it. Imagine yourself just doing what you like. Isn't it wonderful?

- Sure!

- The work is usually a thorn in the human being's side. If people liked what they do, they would be happier, but usually they don't. See the faces of people who pass by the street anywhere in the world. If we look carefully, we will see that their faces express sadness, resentment and disappointment. An insignificant percentage expresses joy, principally because people are conditioned to do what they don't like for a meager wage that is barely enough to pay the basics. They do not have the courage to improve in the area that they really would like to work and also because they fear seeking new things, they discredit themselves, they fear the unknown, they fear investing in something new, which may not work. Anyway, they fear fighting. Hence the almost general frustration. I mentioned the fact about the faces of pedestrians, because when people walk down the street, they are usually alone and are rarely observed, so in those moments they surrender to thoughts and extrapolate feelings through their faces, without realizing it. Still others, not even dreaming, have courage.

- I disagree! Everyone dreams of a better life!

- They dream of the very minimum. For me this is not dreaming! I am going to tell you the story of a friend of mine: He worked for a manual service company. And he always said "one day I will buy a plot of land and build my house". After years of hard work, he bought the plot of land and built his house, but he did so and still earns the meager salary he earned many years ago. Do you know why?

- I don't think so!

- Because he only dreamed it. He never dreamed of a job where he could earn a lot of money so he never did anything to change that situation. He is still fascinated with the success of others, but he sees that success as something that does not belong to him. He will never grow while thinking like that.

- Yeah... You're right!

- Never be afraid of dreaming, because the **dream is the first step towards achievement.** Also don't forget that **just dreaming is not enough. We have to plan every step towards realization and work without laziness and without fear.** Specialization in the area we want to address is indispensable.

- I agree. My father taught me this since I was very young.

- I advised a certain religious leader, very full of faith, but with little spiritual knowledge, to go back to school, since being semi-illiterate he would never grow professionally. He replied that the Holy Ghost would guide him in what he should do and therefore he did not need books. I explained him that he could make a lot of money and be rich if he studied and this way get conditions to help other people. He replied that sacrifices bring blessings. He ignored the very scriptures that say, **"yea, seek ye out of the best books words of wisdom; seek learning, even by study and also by faith" (D&C 88-118).**
He was wrong to think that the sacred scriptures are the only good books.

It is also important to know that when we seek something that we really aspire to, discouragement will not hit us so hard.

- The problem is that many people die old without having discovered what they want in life ...

- It is true! But if we look at what we liked as a child, we will know that there is our aspiration. As a teenager who loves drawing and does not get tired of it, on the contrary, the more he draws, the more he feels the desire to draw and makes well done drawings, he has the gift for this art, and can be a good painter or similar. He who in a simple gesture finds inspiration to compose poetry has the gift of being a poet or a writer. So just observe what attracts you and develop the technique in this specific area and you will meet realization. On the other hand, if we do something, even if we put leisure and soon get tired forget it, because it only serves for leisure. Never to work on a daily basis.

- Wow! Great to meet you! My long trip was worth it. What else?

- Now, I'm going to tell you a very simple little secret regarding the way you must present yourself. Dress up for the occasion. This is halfway to captivating people. Nothing worse than walking badly dressed, dirty, disheveled or unshaven.

Lorecí Ribeiro Farinon, always insisted that a good looking does count a lot! The appearance associated with friendliness and education is almost a sure win! It is much easier to maintain a good looking to change a bad impression generated by carelessness on our part.

- Right. My parents already told me about it.

- Good!

- What to do, when everything seems to go wrong and we are totally in debt?

- Then, find out who the real winners are! Those who don't get discouraged. Usually people get desperate, start treating others badly, alienating customers and making the situation worse. They begin to treat family members badly and thus disintegrate the family. Many, however, remain calm and continue to struggle. They analyze the facts and look for flawed points to eliminate them and thus start to improve the situation. In the financial field, it is sometimes necessary to sell something to pay off debts and thus avoid interest and possible inconvenience. It is also necessary to see why the business is not going well. Perhaps it is a lack of specialization, an area of the market that is very exploited, a final product without interest on the part of the consumer, etc. The entrepreneur has to have the courage to admit that it did not work and leave the business, logically after proving that it really is not worth continuing. This does not mean failure! It means that this entrepreneur has personality and willpower and will probably be a winner. If we analyze the lives of people who have won in life, we will find that they have failed at one time or another, but it is important to never let discouragement show through, otherwise they will lose productivity and their business will definitely be liquidated. The scriptures say that we are gods (John 10:34 and Psalm 82:06). This means that we have divine power within us and certainly if we developed 100% of our mental capacity, we would have the power that God has. Master Jesus Christ often spoke words like: "Your faith has healed you". Your faith! Not God. God has given us the power to do everything, we just need to have faith. **If we believe that we will win and work hard for it, it will be so.**

Something that helps us win is having contacts. **Never fail to make friends. The more you know the better. The more chances you will have of receiving support to carry out an enterprise.** Friendship helps a lot!

When you are talking to someone, listen carefully and try to identify the type of person you are communicating with using psychology. **Try to find out what the person likes and talk about that topic**. Take yourself as an example; think of a friend you like to talk to, and then analyze the type of subject you normally discuss and you will come to the conclusion that you like the same things. Based on this principle, we conclude that we will be able to please the person and they will be interested in the subject and will give us attention. If we approach subjects that a person does not like, we will not be able to captivate her/him and we will not receive attention.

We can conclude that in order to close a deal, make many friends, receive attention, etc., we must give priority to matters that the person we talk to likes. Sometimes it is necessary for a salesperson to find out some private things the customer likes to then touch on that subject and thus make him start to open up to dialogue and later start buying. If we analyze it, we will come to the conclusion that most people address issues they like no matter whether or not the interlocutor is interested in hearing. Whoever does so becomes a boring person in the others vision and fails to captivate many people. This is probably because we have a serious inferiority complex; perhaps to hide our deficiencies better known to us than to anyone else and so we always try to expose something admirable that we have accomplished, no matter if the other person wants to hear it or not. **Listening is very valuable, because in addition to making people appreciate us, we also have a chance to learn, because while we speak, we are not learning, but while listening we learn.** Another very interesting way to learn is to watch movies, search the internet and of course, read. These are some ways to get knowledge that will help us become successful. Through reading we can enjoy the wisdom of the greatest thinkers in ancient history and of our time for just a few coins. Too bad that so many good books serve only to decorate shelves and sometimes are never opened. Too bad that the internet is used for so many useless purposes and television to instill empty philosophies in the minds of the people.

Seek your goal and always have the following in mind: **"There are two things to aim for in life: first, to get what you want; and, after that, to enjoy it. Only the wisest of mankind achieve the second" (Borghild Dahl).** Many people forget to enjoy what they have earned. Each achievement must be enjoyed as soon as we obtain it and for as long as it belongs to us. **Look back and remember your worst days and then you will see how much you have to enjoy.** However, if you are going through the worst phase of your life, remember what you already had and did not take advantage of and use it as a stimulus to seek something you can enjoy in a difficult time of your life.

Perhaps you know this story, as it happens to many. It happened to me too, so I'll tell you. I made a lot of money a few years ago and everything I earned I spent. Much of it in superfluous things, until one day the crisis came. My business went bankrupt, I ran out of work and money. I owed an amount that I would probably never be able to pay. So, what do you think I did?

- I have no idea!

- I looked for a job that would give me a lot of money. I started to improve myself in the computer area. I paid for language courses for the children and photography course for the wife and worked hard. I started to develop my talent as a writer. I wrote a book. I got sponsorship to pay part of the publishing house and I earned money to pay the debts and got rich. Not to mention that soon the children were trained and earning their own money, as well as the wife. In addition, I helped make their dreams come true. The lesson I want you to learn from this is: "**Never say, I'm destroyed, never put limitations on your thoughts, never be too lazy to try to accomplish something that seems impossible to you. Work hard to make things come true. Remember that you can get what you want. Believe in it and work hard for it.**" Now you must go looking for "the most precious diamond of all."

- Thank you so much for everything. But if you have already walked this path and had the dog you also have the treasure! Give it to me please!

- There's more to something than meets the eye. One day you will understand. Go around the world! Start the search where you feel better and if you want to make the job easier, remember that everyone has feelings; they are just like you. **Treat them well, as you would like to be treated.**

- Come on, give me the treasure!

- No one can take my treasure from me! Your treasure is not with me! Now don't waste any more time. Go!

CHAPTER VI

The Valuable Diamond

Sitting in the main square, Dhay thought about how to continue the search. He knew that the treasure was with the wise man, but he did not want to give it to him. Then he remembered the book he had won. He opened it at random and it said: "Your treasure is where your heart is." He thought and thought and suddenly remembered the wise man's advice: "Consult the book and follow in your footsteps". That was it! His heart was in his friends, also in his country of origin, Brazil, and to follow in his footsteps, he would have to go back, along the path he had stepped on. Yes, he would do that. Perhaps the wise man's diamond was no longer the most valuable. Perhaps there was a bigger one in Brazil, or somewhere where he had been before. He headed for the airport. He would go to America. He decided to walk, he didn't know why. Walked ...

Passing in front of a hospital, he met a woman who had just left the hospital and she was crying a lot. He stopped and asked what had happened.

- Sorry lady. Can I help you? What happened?

- It's my son. He needs to have a surgery in order not to die. Otherwise, he will die in a maximum of two days. I don't have the money for the surgery.

The woman burst into tears; nothing could comfort her.

- How much does the surgery cost madam?

The surgery cost the exact sum of money Dhay had.

While Dhay thought about saving that boy's life, he remembered the beggar's advice. He couldn't waste even a cent. He walked a few steps and opened the book: "Thou shalt love thy neighbor as thyself" (Matthew 22:39).

And now, what to do? He knew it was time to spend the last penny he owned... But how would he get back to America? And what would he eat? "No. I can't spend the money," he thought. He headed to the airport; he would not go out of his way.

He stopped in front of the ticket window and thought: "I have to go my way, but what is my way? Maybe it's helping that lady!"

- He returned to the hospital and there was the same lady, sleeping on the bench in front of the hospital.

Dhay knew he couldn't spend the money unnecessarily. But he could argue with the "Enlightened Being". It was a matter of life and death. It needed to be done. He was loving his neighbor as himself! After all, to stay alive he could give up everything else. Life was the most important thing. He would do that to save that child's life. His mission was not more important than the life of a human being!

He called the woman, went into the hospital with her and paid for the surgery. After receiving lots of thanks and kisses from the woman, he left. Now he did not know what to do...

The next day he felt hungry. It was more than twenty-four hours since he had eaten. As he was broke, he decided to go into a restaurant and ask for a dish. He got it but first he had to go to the kitchen to clean the floor, wash dishes and do some other chores, in short, pay for what he was going to eat. Then the restaurant owner gave him a meal worthy of a president.

While eating he made plans. He had to find a way to get back to America. Staying there was complicated. He communicated very poorly in that language.

He had an idea. If he had worked on a plate of food, he could work on a ship that was going to America. His English would help him get a job on a ship in exchange for the trip to America.

However, it was not that simple, he did not even manage to enter the pier. He was stopped by the guard.

He wandered the streets already tired. Calluses on the feet and almost desperate. Those three days sleeping on park benches were not good. Again, he remembered the book which had served as his pillow. As usual, he opened it at random and read: "Wherever your heart is, there will be your treasure". Different page, but the same message. He was looking for the greatest of all treasures, now he knew. There was a clue. It was enough to discover the meaning of the sentence. His chest burned. He didn't know what the phrase meant, but more than ever he was sure this was the right clue.

Suddenly he realized that two men, English by face, were talking on the park bench next door. He began to hear them.

- One thing I learned in life is that **without setting goals we fail.** It is like a man who decides to cross the ocean. He knows the country he wants to reach, but not how to do it. He only knows the destination to reach. He is then launched into the sea in a boat about four meters long and one wide. A stupid act. No supplies, no compass, no intelligence. Will he reach his destination? Just by miracle. Maybe he can get a ride. One chance in a million, in such a vast ocean.

If you ask a hundred entrepreneurs how they intend to achieve their goals, almost everyone will say that they will work hard for it but if you ask what the next step is, they will not know what it is. A war is won by winning many battles. It is for each fight that we must be prepared. Putting your hand on the final goal is just a matter of winning the last battle, but we can only do that if we have won many other battles along the way. Anyone who thinks the life of the winners was easy is wrong.

- We cannot forget that we need to be aware of opportunities, as **opportunities pass "in the blink of an eye", not to mention the fact that they usually come in camouflage.**

- You're right. And it is very important to turn defeat into victory, frustration into personal satisfaction and the weapon for that is optimism and determination.

- Another important point is not to live in Utopia. We have to have our feet on the ground. Dreaming is good and necessary, but the dream must be accompanied by actions, so, yes! It will become real.

- We must also remember that what we do now, helps us to form a firm base for the future. But the past is dead, we cannot live on memories. We also must not procrastinate what we have to do, because we have power over the present, the future, however, may not even exist for us. We can die in the next second, minute, or hour. Who knows when? **The past is gone, the future does not exist, the present is real and tangible, so do what you have to do, now.**

- What I am going to tell you may seem tacky, but it is concrete; My children sometimes criticize me for the possible lack of control on my part, in the face of situations that cause irritation, but they trust me fully, because they never heard from my mouth a single lie.

- It is also worth remembering that not even a battle can be won without courage.

- Yes. And we must also keep our thoughts fixed on our goals, day after day. Thoughts lead to fulfillment. Everything is worked out in the brain to then be executed by our body. Clean up your interior and you'll be a great man. Leave it dirty and it will be useless. We are actually what we think and not what we try to show others. Therefore, we must repel negative thoughts and resentments so that we can ensure the opportunities we have for ourselves. **Many goals are simply overlooked because they have not received due attention.** We also have to concentrate on the subjects. For example, if I decide to become a computer technician, I must first take the following measures: "Make money available for courses, choose the best school, be a totally dedicated student, look for a job to be able to improve myself more and finally when prepared, start the business itself. Then other submissions will come, only then will I become a successful person, which was the main goal."

- Something that brings us down is the fear that sometimes disguises itself as shyness. If we do not face difficult situations and obstacles, we will get nowhere. There is a phrase by an unknown author that I like to use: "Son of God is a god". In its deepest meaning, it means that nothing is impossible for man. Let's look at the following; God created everything that exists and placed us on earth. One of His creations. But before we were, as we are now, literally children of God in spirit. Brothers of Jesus Christ who received a body and took it up in the resurrection, just as we will one day. I mentioned this to make clear, our divine origin, having no intention of preaching religious doctrines, but rather to clarify the foundation of our power. For this I will quote the greatest of all men on the face of the earth. Jesus Christ. And just to leave no room for misunderstandings or misinterpretation on the part of religion, I would like to remind you that I am dealing here with power, not spiritual salvation. For salvation depends on keeping God's commandments, but the power to do things depends on faith. (The certainty that something will or will not happen). Jesus Christ said: "Because you have so little faith. Truly I tell you, if you have faith as small as a mustard seed, you can say to this mountain, 'Move from here to there,' and it will move. Nothing will be impossible for you." (Matthew 17:20). And still for Peter who walked on water He said unto him, "O thou of little faith, wherefore didst thou doubt?" (Matthew 14:31). He wavered in faith and sank. You may think that this was only because Christ, the son of God was there. But I tell you, you are also a child of God. People from different religious backgrounds heal people from incurable diseases. I would like to explain how this occurs. The person who is healed by a clergyman is only healed, if he believes, otherwise he will not be. Power comes from within the person. It comes from the brain that sends the healing message to the offended place and so healing takes place. However, if the person doesn't believe, nothing will happen because person is sending a message to the brain that the sick part will remain sick and so it will be. There are people who do "black witchcraft" against someone, if that someone is not informed of the fact or does not believe, nothing will happen. This is because ignoring or discrediting the fact, the evil message will not be sent to the brain, rendering all the work done useless. But if the person believes, he/she will fear the evil and say to him/herself: "and now, what will I do, that evil will happen to me". So will be.

- That's true. There is a curious fact that happened to me. I was a soccer goalkeeper when I was a child and I had a wart on my elbow and each game pulled it out and it was total torture. It started to grow fast and bigger. My mother had a belief that putting mud on it for seven days it would fall, but it didn't work with me. That's because I didn't believe that would happen. One day, my father took me to the doctor to prescribe a medicine that would kill the so-called wart. I asked the doctor about beliefs; if they worked. I only did it to hear him say it was foolish and to convince my mom and dad that they were wrong to believe it. However, it was my surprise to hear him say it worked. I told him it didn't work with me. He said it only works with those who believe and explained the case to me scientifically. He said that the brain sent the wart destruction message and certain antibodies destroyed it. He then explained to me that as I did not believe, the message of destruction was not sent, but the message that the wart would grow again. I went home and didn't use the medicine, but I told myself. If so, the wart will fall off without medicine and without that belief. So it happened.

- Interesting.

- I made this explanation so that you understand that **if we knew how to use 100% of our mental capacity, we would be similar to God.** We could even create planets, etc.

- **Based on this principle, if you believe that you are capable of making your dream come true, you will!**

- You can be absolutely sure!

Night was already falling when Dhay realized that almost two hours had passed. So, he remembered that he was broke and without food and even with no place to sleep. He thought again of the phrase in the book: "Wherever your heart is, there will be your treasure." That night he would sleep again in the square bench but he decided the next day he would get a job!

Dhay woke up with the first rays of sunlight. His body hurt a lot. The bench was too hard to sleep. Now he knew how bad beggars' lives were. He went to the pier again. He needed work and there on the pier he felt a little closer from home. He had woken up happy because he had deciphered the riddle of the sentence. It was that simple. But he was trying to make things difficult. He woke up with much nostalgia for Brazil. That was where his heart was. In the city of Francisco Beltrão. It was time to go back, he felt. He headed for the dockside entrance.

- Please, sir, I need to work to eat. Is there a job vacancy on the pier?

- I'm sorry. They are all filled at the moment and there is a huge line of people waiting. You won't get anything here.

- Look, I'm from Brazil. I need to earn some money, so that I can return. Can't you help me?

- From Brazil? Do you speak Portuguese?

- Yes. It's my native language! I speak Portuguese and English!

- I have the job you need! Wait here.

The man disappeared into the pier and ten minutes later he returned with someone in uniform, wearing a funny cap. He possibly was the captain of a ship.

- Do you speak Portuguese and English? He asked in poorly spoken Portuguese.

- Yes, sir and a little Spanish.

- Great! Have you ever worked on ships?

- No sir, but I have traveled a lot and have been through many difficult situations and I have always done well. I can do whatever I need. Just explain to me what I am supposed to do and I will do it!

- Very good! A determined boy. I need an interpreter. Something against wearing a uniform?

- Imagine sir! I want to work...

- Very well. Let's go in and let's talk. You will earn good money if you do a good job! The ship leaves for Brazil in five hours.

- Dhay had learned a new lesson; **A frank and enlightening conversation can often change a man's destiny.** Recently, the receptionist told him that there was no chance, as many who arrived before him were waiting for a vacancy and now, he was an interpreter on a ship that would dock in Rio de Janeiro. He would arrive in Brazil soon and with good money in his pocket!

The day was already breaking, the reflections of the sun in the water, made a spectacular view. What a beautiful morning! The most beautiful and happy sunrise ever seen by Dhay. In the distance he could see the statue of Christ the Redeemer. He was home again. He had learned new languages, suffered a lot, but with suffering he had learned new lessons. He really felt like a man for the first time in his life! The world no longer scared him! He had found his dog on the other side of the world and was now looking for the most valuable diamond. He then felt that he would win the great challenge. He would get unlimited power!

Francisco Beltrão, Paraná, Brazil

- Hi dad! Hi mom!

- My son, you came back! Two and a half years have passed! I thought I would never see you again! How I

suffered because your absence!

- Mom, I'm already a man!

- I always said that to your mother! But she still sheds tears. How was the trip son?

- Marvelous, Dad. Hard to believe.

- I see you don't have the dog.

- I already left it in its proper place!

Later on...

- Today we will have a party, to celebrate your return! Tomorrow I want you to meet a great speaker named Edgar Farinon. He says impressive things about relationships, achievements, sales techniques, etc. You will love it!

The next day.
Dependencies of "O Espaço da Arte",
Francisco Beltrão.

The lobby of the municipal theater is gradually being taken over and in a short time it will be full. The place was too small for the number of families, businessmen, doctors and other professionals from the most varied areas, who wanted to hear the lecture of the great Edgar Farinon.

It was an exceptional lecture, and some points marked Dhay forever.

One of the first points cited by Edgar was the way that we could convince people to think like us:

Edgar Farinon:
- If we interview a hundred people, about the last subject they discussed with someone and ask, in their opinion, who was right, we will find that almost all of them will think they were right, or at least say that. Perhaps in the depths of their hearts they admit to being wrong, but out of pride and self-esteem they will not admit it and will argue as far as necessary to defend their opinion. A few do not like to struggle and keep silent or even admit the other person's reason, but deep down they know that they only did it to avoid discussion. They will continue to defend

their way of thinking and will not have changed their minds.

An almost insignificant number of people will analyze both sides and admit deep inside that they are wrong, if they are. So, is it worth discussing when we see that the person does not share our way of thinking? I say no. If not, how will we have harmony together?

The most efficient way is to convince the other person that our point of view is not really ours or that an idea is not ours, but theirs. This logically has to be done subtly, without the person realizing it. If we can convince him that our point of view is not ours, but from him, then he will defend our idea tooth and nail. You may be thinking, but the credit goes to the other person! True, but so what do you want merits or results? Search the results and the merit will be added automatically. If you act in this way, it benefits you, so you win! To do this it is necessary to observe the person. Know his ideas and this is easy, just let him speak. Talking is what most people like to do. Then, subtly, start distorting the person's ideas, filling him with praise for his ideas and he will then be flattered and will end up adopting your idea as his own. But be careful with the dose. It is necessary to explore the right moment and give the right measure of compliments to what the person is saying. Sometimes it is necessary to work day after day, continuous work. This is possible in our home and workplace, for example. Of course, there are situations it is necessary to be fast and dynamic. When we are selling a product and we have a few minutes of attention from the buyer and the buyer tells us that he is not interested, because it's too expensive, if you tell him that he is wrong, he will end of fighting you. He will defend his own idea with all his might. However, if you tell him that he is intelligent and observant, because he initially observed things that other customers do not normally observe and for this reason you will share with him some advantageous facts, you will probably have his attention.

You then explain the product is expensive, because it uses this, that, and other components to guarantee quality, something that other products do not do and that this will bring him greater comfort. If you finish with mentioning a good, well known and influential person who bought the product because he knows that it is important to care for his comfort and the comfort of the family and he preferred to invest (not spend because spending sounds negative), money on useful things and this person when learning about the product didn't think twice and acquired it and finally praised the guy who made the purchase, making it indirectly clear that you admire him for his intelligence.

Your new customer will probably want to be worthy of praise as well and will make the purchase. But first, it is necessary to analyze the client, to know how to approach him, because what may be convincing for one, may be offensive to another.

To know the client, there is nothing like giving him the chance to speak at will, as I said before, and encouraging him with compliments, agreeing whenever possible and when disagreeing, instead of arguing, just remain quiet and just listen to him. Once you know what type of person you are talking to, it is easier to know how to approach the issue at hand.

A piece of advice that is valid for any situation: **don't lie to your customers**, use real examples, because that way the person will end up proving that what you said is true and will bring you other customers. If he sees that you lied to him, he will tell the others and you will lose this opportunity and other possible clients.

Be careful how you act because we judge ourselves by what we believe we are able to do, but people judge us by what we have already done and if we did something unworthy people will probably remember it for the rest of their lives. If we did something good, they will quickly forget.

Take care to **never lose sight of the objective** whether in a lecture, in an interview, in your personal life or in any other situation. **Sometimes we get worried about trivial things, unimportant details and we end up moving away from the goal or when things start to get difficult, we simply choose something easier, thus moving away from our goals. Hence the great number of frustrated people who work in services that they hate, but never have the courage to seek what they dream.**

But how to seek what we dream? Good question, isn't it? I certainly cannot be an economist without first graduating in economics. **The way is to study! Study hard about what we want for ourselves!**

We see the job market, full of poorly qualified, lazy people, who refuse to take a training course, paid by the company they work for and when they take the course, they don't study hard, they miss classes, showing they don't value it, because they got it for free, as if it were worthless because it was free. If they have to pay for the course, they have the excuse of not having money. That way they'll never get anything! They will have a frustrated life. I compare them to some public service employees. They hate what they do and do it for a meager salary, in many cases, but they do not seek a better job, nor do they strive to move up. They are not looking for something better and they still boast of having their work guaranteed because the law doesn't allow the government to fire them. They boast of their own prisons, which they have imposed themselves.

Another factor to analyze is the boss - employee relationship is the fact the boss on the one hand tries to exploit the employee to the maximum and pays him poorly. The employee on the other hand regrets his salary, work, boss, etc. and does not make an effort because he does not own the business. Forgetting that if the company goes bad, he may no longer have his job. Finally, they both forget that "you scratch my back and I'll scratch yours.".

The company will only work well when the boss and the employee work in harmony. The boss forgets that the employee is not a slave, but someone who sells his services. The employee forgets that once the service is sold, it must be rendered efficiently or it will not be entitled to the salary. Anyway, both are wrong.

- Still, **it is necessary to be able to talk on an equal basis with people from different social and professional levels.** For that, the reading of good books is indispensable. We must be regular readers. To perfect ourselves in computers and speak several languages, due to globalization. Today, business transactions are made with any company, anywhere in the world, sitting on a chair inside the office or the library at home, over the Internet. This is the trend of the world market. Whoever does not follow this progress will be finished because the market evolution is very fast. From one month to the next we have news in the area of information technology. Speaking different languages helps. How to communicate with the world without having a common language? Impossible. Be smart! Stay up to date or you will fail. Study! The collective only works well when individuals become aware that each has to do their part.

You may think: Why should I do it if almost no one else does it. I tell you that many think differently from you and are doing their part. It is worth doing. Certainly, those who see you doing your best, will imitate you and thus a chain will be formed, then everything starts to change.

I would like to tell you two stories. Unfortunately, the authors are unaware. But they are very wise stories.

The first, talks about a hummingbird. One day there was a large fire in the forest, and the animals ran away, except for the hummingbird.

On the run, the elephant came across the hummingbird, so tiny a creature. And when it saw the bird flying from the lake to the fire and vice versa it asked the bird what it was doing. The hummingbird told the elephant that it fetched water from the lake and threw it on the fire to put it out. The elephant that could carry much more water if he wanted laughed at the tiny bird and told it that he would never be able to put the fire out with such tiny droplets. The hummingbird replied that he knew this, but it still had to do its part and continued in its work, while the great elephant continued its run.

People like the hummingbird in the story are responsible for the great events in human history. Is that you? Are you the hummingbird or the elephant? You may also think that you will not change anything if you do your little part. I tell you that you are totally wrong. Certainly, many people who are having access to this report of mine, will change their lives and through them others will also be convinced of this and change their lives. I am not the only one in the world to preach and practice this. We are millions.

The other story tells of a people who once decided to build a lake of milk. They built the lake. It just needed to be filled. To this end it was agreed that the next night, the lake would be full and for that, each inhabitant undertook to place a glass of milk in the lake, so the magician of the kingdom would make sure that it never dried out and remained always healthy. That done, the lake would dawn overflowing with milk. However, a certain dishonest guy decided that he would put water instead of milk, as a glass of water in thousands of glasses of milk would never be noticed. And he did that. The next day, everyone was amazed when looking at the lake and seeing a crystalline lake, overflowing with water.

I think this story needs no comment.

There is also the history of a people who crossed the United States of America, from New York, to Salt Lake City, in the State of Utah. Guided by a prophet named Joseph Smith and later by another named Brigham Young. They ran away from those who did not believe in their beliefs and sought a place of peace, where they could worship God in peace and harmony. They crossed rivers and swamps, mountains, forests and deserts. They faced, rain, sun and snow. Whole families, using only wagons, often, in the absence of animals, pulled by themselves. They faced disease, cold, heat, rebels, (who did not accept them), the brave American Indians, thirst, hunger and much more. They established their people in cities that they themselves built in the middle of the American desert.

They built temples and churches and were even repressed by the American government, which felt powerless, due to the humility and goodness of those people. Today there are millions of them in the United States and all around the world. A people who faced the most difficult situations just to be able to be honest; To be able to preach and live divine love on earth. A people who dared to be so faithful that God blessed them to extremes, making them an exemplary and rich people. These people I refer to are without a doubt the most honest and enterprising people on the face of the earth. They are called by the nickname "The Mormons". Even today, they are slandered by envious people who ignore their reality. They are a people for sure, like the hummingbird in the story I told you. They are an example in the world that must be followed, regardless of religious beliefs. The ones who follow their examples for sure will have financial prosperity and material and spiritual well-being.

We have many other examples of resourceful people in the world, Follow them. Always **try to match the best, try to be even better than the best and then this world will be one of prosperity.** Finally, it will be a little piece of heaven on earth.

I have something very important to tell you now. I would like you to pay close attention. It refers to the long staircase that leads to the top. Professional achievement.

The first important detail is that **there is not a single human being who has not already failed on the path of success. Failures happen, but we must not let ourselves be overwhelmed by them.** Certainly, no matter how bad the failure is, it can be taken advantage of. Just look at the whys and mistakes made and look for solutions so that in the future the same mistakes will not be repeated. **Don't be ashamed to move on after a failure. It is shameful to bow. The pain of defeat is better than the shame of never having tried.**

I would like to tell you the story of one of my friends. One day with as little money as possible, he opened his business. He had almost no administrative experience, which is already half a step towards failure, as professional improvement is the minimum that is needed to succeed. There were years of struggles, learning from mistakes. It was a mutual effort from him and his wife. They struggled a lot. They worked in the morning, afternoon and night. His biggest mistake! It was missing the habit of reading, walking hand in hand, playing sports, having fun etc. The fatigue came. The disagreements due to physical and mainly mental fatigue and finally the divorce decision. Deep love had turned into displeasure and pain.

But God blessed them at that time. They managed to sell the business. They inherited some debts that they only finished paying after many years. But they saved the marriage. Day by day, he began to rescue everything they had lost.

He was already in emotional control again and was earning a good salary. His wife still with the branch, was still very tired. She often lost control and insisted on not getting rid of the business. She often accused him of things he didn't do and often spoke of getting divorced. He, however, now much more experienced, kept cool. Catching up on business, but never forgetting leisure. Despite the criticisms of the poor tired woman who accused him of being a vagabond, as she got used to only working.

He then started to analyze why he failed and found out that one blamed the other for his/her own mistakes and never praised the other for his/her successes. That's how love started to fade.

This is typical of people. **The human being, most of the time seeks to hide the error, accusing the closest ones.** The victims are usually family members, partners or employees. In doing so, we despise the fact that the other person when criticized, even with good intentions, puts him/herself in self-defense and automatically starts to act as an opponent. In addition to self-defense, he/she will attack as a form of defense. This then becomes reciprocal, increasing day after day, bringing about the disintegration of a relationship, which until then was beautiful. So don't forget: **Criticism turns friends into enemies.**
On the other hand, **a sincere compliment softens even a heart of stone**. But don't forget that the compliment must

be sincere. To do so, just refrain from criticizing the negative points, just subtly letting on that you don't like this or that, and start praising all possible positive points. This is an honest way of being sincere instead of faking compliments. It is very important, to praise, in presence of a person admired by the one who receives the praise, because that raises the ego and undoubtedly changes his attitude towards you, little by little. This may seem difficult to you, but remember that you always start with the first step and this is usually the most difficult. So go ahead. Take the first step.

Remember a few important points:

Perseverance: Never say I'm done. **Never give up. Remember that discouragement brings down almost everyone. Those who win in life are those who overcome discouragement, who persevere.**

Patience: This allows you to wait for the right time. Things often do not happen, as and when we want. Everything has its time. Be patient, don't forget! **Patience is one of the divine attributes.**

Kindness: **Be good, reach out and this will yield you a multitude of friends and benefits.** Be kind to everyone and you will be admired by many and if you are admired you will be highly favored. Opportunities will abound day after day.

Sympathy: Do you like rude people or do you prefer friendly ones? **Sympathy will make you love the others for their kind of being and that will gain you, their friendship.**

Friendship: Having friends cheers any heart and with the other attributes mentioned many benefits will arise. Almost all the help we receive comes from friends and when we help or are helped by a stranger, certainly a new friendship arises.

Humility: Being humble does not mean devaluing yourself, as many people think, but the other way around. It is putting yourself in the place you are due! Equal place with others. **You are only superior or inferior professionally, but as human beings, as children of God, we are all the same. So, value the next one, because you can find him when climbing, as well as descending on the ladder of life.**

The scriptures bring us a famous phrase: "love thy neighbor as thyself". (Leviticus 19:18). Believe it or not, but that is the great wisdom of the world.

Morning of the following day.

- I thought Edgar's lecture was kind of strange. He mixed human relationship with religion ...

- But there is a connection!

- Ah, father! I don't know, but I confess that I felt something inside me when he spoke of love for our neighbor.

- Love is important and helps us acquire many friends and having many friends is easier to win in life.

- Tomorrow I'll go out looking for treasures again. I already got two. Now I'm going after the third, the most precious diamond in the world.

- Where will you start?

- Do not know. I will ask for help from a guide book that I won. It will show me the way forward.

- Why did you come back?

- I do not know! I followed the heart. I love you, the mother, the friends ...

- Love is really a precious treasure that we have in our lives and I really missed you too.

- Yes, I know! In fact, I don't feel the urge to leave. Maybe I'll stay a little longer.

- Maybe your treasure is here!

- Perhaps! I feel in a good mood. I think something fantastic is going to happen.

Dhay, then decided to read his book and a little disappointed talked to his mother, because he knew that she always had wise advice to give him.

- I tried to find an answer in the book, but I found none. This is very strange!

- What did you read? Asked his mother.

- I read a love story, between parents and children and friends. It happened in a neighborhood without violence, where if someone found something on the street, he would give it back to the owner and everyone would help each other. Pure utopia.

- There must be some sense! Let's think about it ...
The next day Lucia talks about Beto, a neighbor who needs help with the house painting.

- Beto, our new neighbor, from the front house is in need of help to paint the house. You are good at it. Could you help him?

- Of course. After all, doing a favor makes me happy.

A week later.

- The house looks beautiful! Doesn't it?

- Yes! It is wonderful! But tell me, have you decided on where to start the search for the treasure?

- No! I've been reading the book all week long. The first three days I opened it at random and the three times I opened it on the page of that love story. On the fourth and fifth day I opened it taking care to open it in different places. On the sixth and seventh days I thought of a number and opened it.

- And then?

- All times different stories. All love stories. Now I feel I must not insist on opening the book anymore and look for the answer somewhere else.

His mother then decided to tell him what she had been thinking for some time.

- Son, I was analyzing what you told us about your trip around the world. You have shown love for many people. The sage has shown love for you and has advised you to seek the most valuable diamond. You came back to Brazil and in the lecture, Edgar Farinon talked about love. You didn't charge anything for painting Beto's house. You did it for love and finally, for a week the book showed you only love stories ...

- So, what mom?

- So, I want you to think. What treasure are you looking for?

- The most valuable treasure in the world.

- And the sage hasn't found him yet?

- Yes. But he didn't want to give it to me. He said that I would have to find my own treasure, because that was his!

- But the most valuable treasure is singular and not plural, so there is only one!

- That I haven't been able to understand yet!

- And what is the most valuable treasure in the world?

- I do not know. I think it's a giant diamond!

- But the wise man told you he would keep his and you would have to get yours. How is it possible if there is only one?

- I found out, mother! There are two equal treasures. With exactly the same value!

- No son! There is only one treasure!

- Can you be clearer? I do not understand!

- You traveled the world and you were guided by the sage. You have also been guided to the plant store and finally to the pot with the Guachuma. Finally, you have been guided back home not to mention the fact that you had many chances to prove your love.

- Okay, mom, so what? Spit it out...

- Your treasure is spiritual and not material. What do you think it can be?

- Sure! Love! Mommy, you are brilliant! If so, I will have already found three treasures! This is awesome! The book will confirm whether it is or not true. I'll check.

Dhay ran to his room and opened the book at random and his eyes hit a phrase, just below the middle of the page that said: "A mother's advice is a right path that only wise people can take!"

He had discovered the third treasure! Now it was time to find out which one was next.

That night in a quick appearance the "Enlightened Being" told him that the next treasure was "the seedling of the noblest tree." He didn't give Dhay a single clue on how to get it. It made him impatient, but he had no choice because the "Enlightened Being" just showed up when he wanted to, not when he was called.

Dhay said goodbye to his parents again.

- I will seek the seedling of the noblest tree and I know where to find it.

- Where are you going to find it?

- Temples built to worship God used cedar from Lebanon, as it is the most noble wood. I will go there and find the most beautiful seedling!

- Son! Are you going to cross the world again? Asked his mother.

- I must. But this time it will be quick. I have a right destination and I know what I'm looking for. It will be easy.

CHAPTER VII.

The Seedling of the Most Noble Tree.

Three days later.

Guarulhos - São Paulo International Airport.

Inside the plane, Dhay met a rather interesting man. A long beard, down to his stomach and a somewhat suffered appearance, showing old age, but a very strong man physically and also very determined.

- Where are you going boy?

- New York, then Lebanon.

- I will stay in New York.

- Do you live there?

- No. Salt Lake, Utah.

- Really?! I've been there. Very beautiful city and very hospitable people.

- Yes! There the hand of God rests.

-I think so. Ingenious people, that one and also very affectionate.

- Yeah. You're right...

- It caught my attention that in many markets neither cigarettes nor alcoholic beverages are sold. I also found Salt Lake interesting. It is isolated in the middle of the desert, around a lake with salt water!

- The city also offers other tourist attractions.

- I met a very interesting young man in the Mormon Temple square. We chatted for hours. I learned a lot that day. Sitting there I felt a great inner peace. Maybe that's why I liked that place so much.

- I'll give you my address, if you ever go back there, visit me. Take time to know the city and the people well. You may never want to leave.

- Okay! If possible, I will go.

- Just go. **We should always put recreational activities in our day to day. This eliminates fatigue.** Many families sometimes disintegrate by just working.

- It is true. Sometimes little things make a big difference.

- You're a smart young man. I feel that you will be great. Never forget your goals, however distant they may be, or however difficult they may be. Go ahead. Draw intermediate goals. This helps to achieve the goal.

Have you ever made bread?

- No sir.

- Let's suppose you want to do it. It looks difficult and complicated. But what do you think of putting milk in the bowl?

- Easy.

- And mix the eggs with the milk?

- Easy.

- So are all the other steps. If you think about them individually and execute them one by one, without thinking about how far the final goal is, when you realize it, everything will be finished. So never forget your goal. Never give up of it.

- So... I always do that and it helps a lot. **It is also important to have a view of the consequences of what we are going to do. For sometimes it is not profitable to carry out what we have in mind. We must always measure the pros and cons.**

- Ah! Yes. We must have initiative and a global vision. It is also sometimes necessary to delegate functions instead of doing everything yourself. This is called teamwork and the boss's role is to delegate functions and not only perform them.

When we are in a position to rule or even if we are subordinates, we have to be very careful with what we speak. "A shut mouth catches no flies". It is better to stay quiet instead of talking and hurting another person, who will become an enemy, although sometimes for any reason the person doesn't show it. To captivate people, we have to treat them in a way that doesn't hurt them. We must also work our ideas in a subtle way because sometimes people can put themselves against their own principles just to not admit you are right.

- Are there people like that?

- Sure. Most people also love to tell what they do sensationally, as a way of self-worth. When we don't pay attention to what they are saying and insist on keep talking, instead of listening, they simply get closed, not paying attention to what we are saying, either. This way the conversation doesn't bring good results and one will not like the other and vice versa. If we listen to them, they will probably like us and start admiring us.

- It is also important to take care of what we say, because sometimes our enemies are "dressed in sympathy masks", just trying to extract something that they can use against us. "They are wolves in sheep's clothing."

- I'm going to give you some tips on how to manage, because for sure, one day they will be useful:

1 - Adapt to different situations. Act in a way that pleases people, but do not let yourself be dominated and **act with sympathy and calm or with rigidity and authority, as the occasion requires, but never be exalted**. If necessary to impose your authority, do so without losing control and without shouting.

2 - **If your employees are not efficient, train or replace them, otherwise your enterprise will sink.**

3 - Make well-studied decisions, so that they do not bring undesirable consequences to you and always try to be aware of everything to be able to make immediate and correct decisions when the occasion demands, because sometimes postponing something will bring disastrous consequences.

4 - The leader must be good and friendly, but energetic, as to the fulfillment of his orders. **The employee must act immediately and perfectly and never postpone what must be done immediately.** Pretend that the boss's business is yours, so if he doesn't value you, another company will see your effort and will do it. (The news about excellent employees arrives to other companies one or other way.) Then you will grow quickly.

5 - Beware of difficult times. When everything seems lost, it is the most important time to remain calm and not rush into attitudes.

- Wow! We're arriving in New York! It was nice to talk to you. Thank you for the tips.

- God bless you! And don't forget. Always look for what is good and virtuous, and stay away from everything that is impure.

Beirut - Lebanon.

- Good morning, sir!

- Good morning!

- Can you tell me if there are any cedar trees around here?

- Yes! This tree beside us is a cedar.

- Thank you, sir!

Dhay went to the tree, there were some seedlings, but how could it be so easy? Something was wrong! It was then that he saw a sign saying "don't step on the grass". How could he get a seedling when couldn't step on the grass? He looked everywhere. Nobody was looking. He hesitated, as he always tried to be pure in thoughts and actions and also because he didn't know the laws of the country and the consequences. So how would he go ahead taking the seedling without breaking the rule? If he broke it, he would be breaking the law and consequently he would be being impure and also could have problems. He decided to look for another cedar seedling. Now he knew a Lebanese cedar.

He decided to have lunch before continuing his search. He was exhausted and hungry.

After a very exotic lunch, (Samke Harrah) compared to Brazilian food, he decided to visit the city and at the same time seek his cedar seedling.

Everything was going well, there was no problem, as Lebanon has English, Arabic and French as official languages and English was evidently not a problem for him.

The Archaeological Museum

His concentration on those ancient human bones was broken, by the soft voice of a woman who in English spoke to him.

- Fascinating museum, isn't it?

-!? Ah yes, incredible things ...

- I'm Lyn. You are not from here. Are you?

- No! I am American! From Brazil!

- Soon I imagined. The face of the American people is unmistakable. I am also from there.

- Are you here for tourism?

- Yes.

- Where you are from?

- Oakland, California. Have you ever been there?

- No. Maybe one day ...

- What's your name?

- Dhay.

- Where in Brazil are you from?

- Francisco Beltrão, Pr. In the south of the country.

- I never heard of it.

- Small town.

- Traveling with the family?

- No. I'm alone.

- Me too.

- Oh, really? Gosh! And your parents?

- They're in America.

- I know ... How about we have dinner together?

- Why not! I would love to.

Later in the Al Halabi Restaurant.

- When are you going back to America Dhay?

- I really don't know. But for sure in a few days.

- Straight to Brazil?

- I think so. Speaking of it... Have you ever been to Brazil?

- No.

- You're invited.

- OK! Maybe one day...

- Wouldn't you like to visit the rest of the city in my company?

- You know I do! When I saw you, I was sure it was very important to meet you. Don't ask why, because I don't really know. But there is a reason. I'm sure!

- Wow! What an honor!

- It's not flattery. I always follow my heart.

- I felt the same and I know it's not because you are splendidly beautiful!

- Flatterer, shameless!

- It is true! Too bad we won't be together much longer.

- Yeah...

- What do you think of Islam?

- Everyone has free will, I respect them, but I'm a Christian. What about you?

- I also believe in God and Jesus Christ, but I don't go to church normally.

- I go every Sunday.

- I think you're right... What hotel are you staying at?

- At Hilton Beirut Metropolitan Palace!

- I'm at the Mediterranean Hotel. Who will move? You or me?

- I prefer to move. I didn't like the hotel. However, separate rooms. Religious issue. I hope you can understand.

- Sure! I intend to marry a woman like that!

- I'm serious.

- Me too. I intend to know you better!

- Okay, well, I'll give you my address in America.

- Do you have boyfriend?

- No.

- In that case I promise to stay in touch. Internet, telephone ...

- Nice! Could you help me with my bags?

- Sure!

The sun came up beautiful, worthy of a postcard. Dhay woke up and the first thing he thought of was to knock on Lyn's door, to enjoy that magical moment together. At that moment, someone knocked on his door. There she was, dressed like a princess for her prince. A long kiss and there they were admiring that wonderful sunrise. Half an hour later they shared breakfast. Back in the room Lyn notices the book that has accompanied him on his trips.

- What book is this?

- Advice for everyday life. By the way, I have to go back to Brazil.

- I'm going to Israel. Come with me?

- I'll think about it!

Several days passed and Dhay living the delights that dating provided him did not realize that his goals had been set aside.

Then he read in the book: **Do not deviate from your goals. Always keep them alive in your soul. Nothing should stop you.**

Yes. It was time to move on. But Dhay knew deep inside that Lyn hadn't come by chance and he knew he hadn't wasted any time up to now. However, it was time to say goodbye.

He said goodbye and got back to his search for the cedar seedlings because he knew that the most noble species of cedars were found in Sidon. He took the first flight and left the capital Beirut.

He arrived in Sidon in the early evening and went to a hotel. Lying in bed, he started thinking about life and started to think about the crazy things in his life all because he had known the "Enlightened Being". He wondered why so few could get to know him. He was sure that the words spoken by his friend Rudimar Olkoski were true: **"People are afraid of dreaming!"** It was true, the human being is funny. He thinks: "Ah, if I were that guy, I would be very happy". But they dare not dream of achieving their own desired success. They think that this joy is possible only for others.

Immersed in his thoughts, he remembered Raul Seixas. Considered the greatest rocker of all time in Brazil. He left Bahia and suffered a lot and he certainly thought about giving up, many times, but neither hunger, nor cold, nor fear, made him stop dreaming. Thanks to that, he reached the top.

One point to consider is that nothing happens by chance. Everything goes through our brain before we practice it. Even what we do, instinctively and even by the reflexes. Based on this scientifically proven fact, we conclude that it is necessary to dream in order to achieve something. So, **dream and fulfill yourself or be afraid to dream and be frustrated.**

However, there are different ways to dream.

There are those who dream and do nothing to make the dream come true. This is commonplace. They just stay in theory. They are afraid of practice. Typical of losers.

There are those who dream and make plans to make the dream come true and work hard to make it come true. They "go through hell" as the saying goes. I am sure that people who do not dream have no chance of fulfilling themselves. Those who are afraid of dreaming and therefore rarely dream, also have no chance of success.

From those who are daring to dream and work for it, few are realized. Why? Because they don't use enough intelligence to do so. Success requires more than work, requires hard work and much study in the specific area what few do. It requires cunning, humility, perseverance. You can never lack patience and inner strength to always get up when you fall, (many people do not get up even from the first fall). However, a successful life means giving and courage to rise a thousand times if necessary. Contrary to what many people think, success is not about winning over winning. **All successful human beings accumulate defeats in their careers. But they know how to lift their heads and start again.** They know how to envision the final victory and **use their own defeats as experiences.** They become strong and reach the top they dreamed of.

The day dawned and Dhay woke up with the sound of a thunder. It was a storm that had not been seen like that in a long time. He decided to go downstairs for breakfast.

It was the first breakfast in Sidon and the table looked empty without Lyn at his side.

After breakfast Dhay went to the lobby to read the newspapers. Concentrating on reading, Dhay only realized that a man sat beside him when he addressed him.

- Good morning sir!

- Good morning!

- Looks like you're an American ...

- Yes sir.

- Where from?

- Brazil.

- Brazil? I know Rio de Janeiro, a beautiful city.

- It is true!

- On business?

- No. Tourism!

- I am a top minister here in Lebanon.

- ...

- I have a business to offer you.

- Ok. I am interested in knowing about that ...

- I have a certain amount of dollars. Budget left over. Normal thing. However, I have no way to justify entering my accounts. So, I need to make a deposit abroad and then redeem it as income from companies there so there is no control and the entry is justified.

- I'm sorry, sir. This goes against my principles.

- Sum of twenty million dollars. 33% is for you! Only on the first bank deposit. This transaction can be done with some frequency. Soon you will be a billionaire! It is an easy game, without risks. You open accounts in different countries, so everything is camouflaged. Small amounts in each account. You do not need to do anything. You only provide us with account numbers and make withdrawals from us and passes on to us. Operating expenses and taxes are on me. Your total is net! Only chance in life!

- No, thank you! Now, if you'll excuse me ...

Dhay then went to his room and was somewhat thoughtful. It was a unique chance, really, to get rich overnight. But that was dishonest business. How many did not die of hunger, disease, cold, lack of support? And the government is stealing their lives by embezzling tax money. He tried to forget the subject.

He then decided to check his book again. He felt a little worried. That trip was supposed to be a day or two in Lebanon and weeks had passed and he had not completed that simple mission.

He had learned a new lesson. **Things sometimes seem simple, but they can be much more complex than they show. So, all the diligence can be little. We should never underestimate anything or anyone.** One minute of distraction and we may have thrown it away a lifetime. Total attention is paramount.

He read in the book that who is clean of hands and pure in heart will receive the Lord's blessings:
" ³ Who shall ascend into the hill of the Lord? Or who shall stand in his holy place?

⁴ He that hath clean hands, and a pure heart; who hath not lifted up his soul unto vanity, nor sworn deceitfully.

⁵ He shall receive the blessing from the Lord, and righteousness from the God of his salvation." (Psalm 24: 3-5).

He was right, he had acted correctly. Being pure was important to him since childhood.

The day dawned beautiful and Dhay got up early, before daylight. He was cheerful and willing to find his cedar.

He walked towards the central square and felt the urge to sit there. For two hours an inner voice asked him to remain in that place.

Suddenly he found himself in front of a boy with a pistol in his hand and was informed that it was an assault. He did not react. He delivered everything. Holding the pistol discreetly in his pocket, the kid forced Dhay to go to the bank and withdraw all his money. He only had five hundred dollars left in the hotel.

Dhay returned to the hotel and when on his way back he met the minister who he had spoken to at the hotel. He resisted the temptation to speak and went ahead.

Arriving at the hotel, lunch was already being served. He sat close to a window from where he could see the skyline and plunged into thoughts. He needed to decide what to do. There were more treasures to be won. Not to mention the cedar seedling.

The restaurant was already full when Dhay realized that a man in a suit and tie was there. He came over and asked if he could sit on the other side of the table. He sat down, asked for something to eat and after a few minutes he started talking to Dhay.

- Where are you from?

- Brazil.

- Really!? I'm from there too! Where in Brazil?

- Francisco Beltrão, Paraná.

- I'm from Cascavel. We are neighbors!

- Wow! The chances of meeting someone from the same region in such a distant place are minimal.

- I'm a businessman. I'm here on business. What about you?

- Tourism.

- Liking it?

- Oh, yes. It's really fun. I even got a girlfriend. She is from the United States. She is in Israel now. Maybe one day I'll visit her. But I'm trying hard to forget about it. The distance is very great and basically, we are stuck with the country in which we live.

- Do not worry. **If something is to be yours, no one can take it from you except yourself.** If you want something, do everything to have it and decree in your subconscious that it will be yours and so it will. But if you do not give importance, it is the same as decreeing that you do not want it and you will lose it. Work hard with will and faith and you will have everything you want.

- It's possible!

- It is right! **Lindolf Bell said** a very wise phrase. **"Smaller than my dream, I can't be!" Much of our talent is wasted for lack of audacity.**

Sorry, am I disturbing you with my talk?

- Go ahead. Listening is a gift I have!

- Success comes with failures. When I sat at this table I did it because, by your worried expression I realized that something bad had happened to you. No one is successful in all situations. Bad things happen throughout our lives, but many of these things come for our good. Can I help you with something?

- No! But I'm still grateful! I'm just a little sad because I was robbed and almost ran out of money, but that's not a problem for me. You can be sure that tomorrow I'll be fine. Right now, I was making plans to get money to return to Brazil since the boy cleared my bank account, but I really don't want you to worry about me. I know how to overcome this kind of problem.

- Do not despair, because everything is resolved in due time. I suffered a financial failure and became totally indebted. Only then I found out how easy it had been to make money and how badly I invested my money. Only then I discovered that if I had saved, I could have a small fortune, but I hadn't. When the crisis came and I bankrupted I started to work hard and pay my debts little by little and today I am doing very well and I learned to save is important. Your case is different, but it makes me think. This will serve as a strength to cheer you up the next time you're in trouble. There is an American saying that I like a lot: "Never say die". (Never get discouraged). **Mood is the driving force that takes us to the top. Remember: "No one can achieve success for you". (Jo Couder).** If you work hard you will win.

I always remember Spencer W. Kimball. He was a great speaker and he was hoarse. He was not afraid. He overcame the problem. He spoke so well that his hoarseness was ignored by the profound message he left for the people who listened to him.

Many seek happiness in fame. I, however, tell you that fame is not exactly success.

- What is success for you?

- Success is being able to do what you like the way you like it. Success is being happy. And for that you have to do what you like. Find out what you really like to do and work with it and you will have discovered the essence of success. Remember also that we must not be frightened by failures, because, as I said before, this is part of the way to success. We must learn lessons from these and continue towards realization. Do what makes you happy and you will know what happiness is.

- You're right. This reminded me of a phrase by Dale Carnegie: "I felt defeated by not having shoes, until one day I met a man who had no feet."

- Yes ... **just look to the side and you will know how much we are blessed.**

-A public speaker named Edgar Farinon said something that struck me: "**We have to focus on the right things and make them the basis for fixing the wrong ones**, instead of clinging to what goes wrong and living in self-pity and letting them spoil what's right".

- Yeah, he's right. Schopenhauer also, said a great truth: "**We always think about what we don't have, but never about what we have. This is the great misfortune in the world**".

- I see that you also have the habit of reading. Congratulations. **Only good readers can acquire enough knowledge to become great. Through reading we can share the great truths told by the greatest geniuses who passed over the earth and perfect this knowledge by making us wise as well.** Reading is one of the good things in life. Only those who acquire this habit can understand the depth of these words. It is worth enjoying this benefit granted to everyone for free. Borghild Dahl said well in his book "I wanted to see". He said that **there are two goals in the life of human beings! The first is to get what we want and the second is to enjoy what we got**" and he added with a sentence that I have written on a note stuck to the wall of my library, right in front of my eyes on the desk: "**Only the wisest people enjoy what they have achieved**". I often complained to myself about the life I have until I learned to see the life I had in the past. Gradually I was achieving everything I always dreamed of, but I didn't realize it. I continued to regret what I didn't have yet, without realizing what I had already acquired. For example, when my wife and I got married, we had a backpack each, a little bit of money in the pocket that was enough for a month's food and a month's rent. At the time I dreamed of owning a big house, with a library and a living room with comfortable sofas. I only came to love lying on the couch or studying in the library, a year after I acquired these things. Simply, lost in my dreams, I forgot to enjoy what I already had. I only realized this when I read the phrase that Dahl quoted. I always observe and see that most people, in the desire to acquire more, forget to enjoy what they already have! I do not allow myself to fall into this error.

But tell me: what's your name?

- Dhay.

- I'm José. Nice to meet you!

- I'm at 504, if you want to continue the conversation show up tonight.

- Okay! See you in the evening.

Later in apartment 504.

- Dhay, tomorrow I'm going back to Brazil on the 21:00 flight. When do you plan to return?

- As soon as possible! At the latest next week.

- Can I help you? I'll pay you the expenses back.

- Okay! I'll give you back soon.

- Imagine! This is nothing.

- ...

- Are we traveling tomorrow?

- Perhaps. I need to pay a visit to a cedar planter and then I'm free.

- Very well. Here is the amount needed to cover the expenses back. If you can, it will be a pleasure to travel with you but otherwise, have a good trip! Pay for the favor I am doing to you by helping someone in need.

- It's ok! Here is my card. If you need to find me.

- Here's mine. If you can, come and meet my family in Cascavel.

- Thanks for everything. God bless you!

Now Dhay already had the money for the trip, he just lacked the cedar seedling.

Dhay walked all day long and found many cedar trees, but no seedlings. He also looked for a place to buy seedlings, but did not obtain this information. How could it be? In the country of cedars, not getting a single seed. He considered himself a failure.

He thought of returning to Brazil and getting a job and living a normal life. It was all so tiring at times ...

He decided to search for information in the book again: "We are what we think", was the written phrase, the only one on the page.

Dhay then thought: Well. I'm a loser! I'll give up!

He dropped the book and threw himself on the bed. He would depart on the first flight. All those difficulties since he first met the "Enlightened Being" was making him tired.

Dhay fell asleep and only woke up the next day. He looked at his watch. This was 8:30 am. He got up, took a shower and got ready to travel. He kept his things in his bags and when he went to get the book, he realized that it was no longer open on the page he had read the day before. How it changed, he couldn't know. Probably the wind, since it had landed near an open window. On page twenty-seven, a phrase popped into his eyes: "**Persistent effort is the point between success and failure**".

He sat on the bed. "I need to reassess the situation. Perhaps I should persevere", he thought. Maybe the phrase, "We are what we think", meant that we had to change the way we think.

Maybe we should see ourselves as winners and not as losers. Perhaps he could overcome this obstacle. In the worst case, he would run out of money and would have to work again to earn it and return to Brazil.
He prayed with great faith; he knew that whoever believes everything is possible. **"And all things, whatsoever ye shall ask in prayer, believing, ye shall receive"**(Matthew 21:22).

He went down to the cafeteria and after breakfast went to the hotel reception to talk with the receptionist for a while before continue his search. When he looked at the receptionist to greet him, his eyes popped out. There was a beautiful and imposing cedar sapling in the decorative vase.

- Young man, could you sell me that cedar seedling?

- I'm sorry, but it's part of the reception decoration.

- I can pay well for it. I really liked it.

- I'm sorry, it's not for sale at all.

- But ...

- Not even, it's the hotel's. Not mine.

- It's ok. Can I know where you bought it?

- I did not buy. I planted it. I don't know anyone who sells cedar seedlings.

- Where did you get the seed?

- Ah, that's easy. Two months from now, all the trees will be full of seeds.

- Wow! I would like to leave today and I cannot wait but I would love to have a tree like this!

- No problem! Wait a minute.

Within three minutes the receptionist returned with a package in hand.

- Here it is. It has at least thirty seeds. I can harvest more for myself if I want.

Dhay was excited. He was giving up after making all efforts. Only one last step was missing. It was true, persistent effort is the point between failure and success and he was what he thought: A successful man.

CHAPTER VIII

The Working Bee.

Dhay left the hotel and went to the square where he had been mugged. He sat on the same bench and began to think, whether he would return to Brazil or not.

He decided to consult the book to find out if he should go back or not and to find out what the next treasure could be. He opened the book and read: In the nectar of the plant, I feel the sweetness of my love that is nearby.

He thought about it. He couldn't understand that message, it seemed to be in code.

He thought of Lyn. It could be her, his love. Nectar was about the bee, but his love was North American and America was a long way away.

He walked around and passing in front of a bar he heard someone singing. He had an idea. He would not return to Brazil until he could understand the message of the book. He decided to increase his cash. He sought service in some bars and after four hours and several establishments visited, he was hired to play in a bar frequented by couples. He ended up staying there for a whole month.

Already with good money in his pocket and very happy, being able to play again.

He fell on the bed of the hotel where he was and felt that it was time to open the book again. There it was written: So hard they work, sweet little bees, but your love that you try to forget, is now far away.

Now everything was very clear. Lyn was very close to Lebanon. She was in Israel. Now she was gone, she should have gone back to America.

He felt a little sad. He could have seen Lyn again, if he had understood the message initially. But what would it mean "So hard they work, sweet little bees"?

TEL-AVIV

Imperial Hotel.

Dhay checked in the Imperial Hotel, took a shower, ate something and decided to go out and visit the city. He visited some museums, his passion. He went to musical instrument stores and tourist spots in the city. During his visits he learned about bee keepers. He discovered that people knew nothing about bees but that in Jerusalem there was a beekeeper. Small business! He only discovered it because he met a boy from there, on his visit to a museum. He stayed a week in Tel-Aviv, and visited many neighborhoods in the city. He searched on the Internet and found some small beekeepers in Jerusalem and headed there.

Arriving in Jerusalem, he met a man who was a speaker and decided to attend his lecture that night.

There he learned things that would be used for the rest of his life. With these words, the speaker expressed his ideas and knowledge:

- Dear sirs, dear ladies, my speech today is based on the words of memorable names, but before I start, I want to remind you that according to scientists, the human being does not use more than 8% of his mental capacity. With 8%, how can a man calculate the mental capacity? How will we be able to calculate the total human capacity and then arrive at denominator 8?

The scriptures also say that we are gods (John 10:34), so as such we can create worlds, etc. I believe that this means using 100% of the mental capacity that God, our Heavenly Father has given us. Based on this principle, we may not use even 1% of our total capacity!
I only cite this fact so that you understand that our power, for human understanding, is unlimited and everything we believe will undoubtedly be realized. "Jesus said unto him,

If thou canst believe, all things are possible to him that believeth"! (Mark 9:23).

What I am going to talk about here is neither dream nor fantasy, it is real!

Dale Carnegie spoke of how to make things happen: "**We need to have a deep and dynamic desire to learn** and a strong determination to increase our ability to deal with people."

Yes! You conquer the hearts then you will have conquered the world! If you hurt a heart it will be closed to you and everything that depends on it you will not achieve, so be helpful. Be a friend. Be faithful. Treat others as you treat yourself and you will achieve everything in life.

Dale also suggests that we must do a weekly analysis of events and write down the mistakes made. We must analyze and seek to know the right way that we should have acted instead so that in the future we will know how to act in a similar situation.

This is very important because if you observe we make the same mistake and as our ancestors. Do you know why? Because we don't get advice from our elders and because we always think we own all the truth.

Criticism is a great evil that afflicts our society.

At night, when you get home, analyze the situations you discussed with someone and count in how many you admitted to have made a mistake. Probably none!

John Wanamaker comments that criticism puts the other side on the defensive, making him not admit the mistake. Criticism hurts the pride of others. I tell you; **it is a thousand times better to be silent than to criticize**. However, whenever possible praise, because praise softens any heart and makes the other person try his best to do what is right in order to receive more praise.

If you want to change someone, don't criticize. Don't forget that we all make mistakes, so let's start changing ourselves. Do you find it difficult? It is much more difficult to change someone else against his/her will!

Benjamin Franklin conquered people's hearts with his sympathy. Do you know what his principle was? **Do not speak bad things of anyone and say everything good that you know of each person.** Try it! Very early you will reap the results.

Imagine being praised by someone who judges you ten years younger! Yeah, we all like to be praised. Praise and turn enemies into allies and friends into brothers. Praise is one of the most powerful weapons we have. It is useful in any situation. Imagine your biggest enemy. He sees you getting involved in a car accident and then in court he says, "He was the one to blame. I saw it. You would hate him even more. Isn't it true? Now, imagine him saying, "He caused the accident, but it was not on purpose. I could see him doing everything possible to prevent it, but despite his best efforts, he couldn't. He's a good man and tried not to hurt anyone." Wouldn't you love him in that moment? Wouldn't you forget your grudge and shake hands in a gesture of friendship? Wouldn't you be forever grateful to him for putting your acquittal?

Well ... **If you don't have anything good to say, stay quiet!** After all, the fact that the other's mistakes are different from yours does not make you any better!

Now I will tell you a true story: A certain employee in a certain company was the best in his job, undoubtedly. However, promotions were given to colleagues infinitely inferior in quality of work. Do you know why? Because they knew how to captivate the leader better than him! Now I give you some advices: Analyze people, including superiors, in your work. Find out how to treat them the way they like. Then you will be successful. Of course, you should always try to be the best professional but it is also essential to captivate your superiors. I mean being docile and helpful to people.

To prove that what I say is true I want you to think about the friend you like the most... Now think about what you two talk about... how this person treats you and how you treat him/her ... Now think about what you like to talk about the most and how you would like to be treated by everyone ... I have no doubt that the treatment received from your friend and the subjects usually covered are exactly the same as you appreciate. Because of that you consider that person your best friend!

Give people what they would like to have, treat them as they would like to be treated, tell them what they would like to hear then you will be inside their hearts and receive everything you want from them.

On the other hand, talk about what a certain person hates, insist on it day by day, treat him like he doesn't like to be treated, forget to praise him for his deeds and you will have conquered a perfect enemy. That person will never give you a single chance for progress.

Worst of all, many people do just that. They hate the boss, and unknowingly they let it show. A chain is only as strong as its weakest link. There goes the employee for another miserable job and there comes another to succeed in his place.

Now I will speak to the leaders because I know that the majority here are superior to someone. Let me start with the words of Charles Schwab: "There is no more skillful way of killing a man's ambitions than criticism by his superior. I never criticize anyone. I believe in the incentive that a man is given to work so. I'm always looking forward to praising. But I am loath to discover faults. If I like something, I am sincere in my approval and lavish in my praise."

Do it and you will be pleased to see your subordinates dedicating themselves more and more and you will have a primordial staff.

This also applies at home. **Criticism is present in 100% of broken marriages**. Do you want conquer the spouse' love? Praise!

I will tell you something based on scientific facts: The woman has many ways to show love. One is keeping the house clean, buying presents, etc. However, they do not clearly show their love. They expect the husband to notice it. He, on the other hand, almost never perceives, as it is man's nature, not to see details. Men see everything as a whole.

The man, by the other hand, usually expresses his love through sex (it's his nature and he can't change it) and working hard to provide for the family. He doesn't care if he will be hungry, but he works hard day by day to give the best to his loved ones.

The woman by nature, does not perceive this form of love and thinks that the great desire for sex on the part of the husband is only to put carnal pleasure. Nothing further from the truth! These are some ways for each other to express love.

Praise, appreciate, acknowledge your spouse's effort and you will get love and attention back.

One last observation. Public praise is the final blow to conquest! The other person will feel valued and will never forget.

On the contrary, public criticism will make the other hate you!

I talked so much about compliments. Let me emphasize; when I speak of praise, I mean something that comes from the heart. Watch out for flattery. This is not a compliment and the person who receives it has an instinct that identifies it. Flattery instead of helping gets in the way. Search within your soul for something that is worthy of praise in the other person and praise them. Do not criticize and do not flatter. Silence is a thousand times better than lying!

Dale Carnegie, quotes in his book "How to Win Friends and Influence People" the fact that **when we want something, we have to show the advantages that the other person will have by helping us**, and not the ones that we will have. For example, if you are looking for work, after all you have debts, family to support, etc. Cite the advantages that the company will have hiring you to have real chances of being hired. What I say with conviction is that most people do not do what helps others, but what helps him/herself. If the company decides to hire you, it is because it needs you, not because you need it. To achieve something, show the advantages that the person or company, if the case, will have if done as you wish and you will have great chances of success.

This requires a little psychology. It is necessary to understand what the other person thinks and craves and then subtly show him that you can give him what he seeks. To do so, sometimes you just have to let the person speak, be a good listener and ask the right questions at the right time. Then show that you can provide what the person needs. If the other person realizes that you are going to give him what he wants, then you have already conquered him and you will get what you want in return. The proverb says: "It is through giving that we receive". Everything is a matter of exchange. Only lazy people just want to receive and they don't grow in life.

Sharing is a great way to make friends. People will only admire you when they realize that you are able to share something. I have a very clear example: a certain young man moved to another city and arrived at the Evangelical church to which he belonged and he felt a little embarrassed because he didn't know anybody. Upon arrival, a "brother" came to welcome him, and began to talk. Soon after, three or four others came to talk to him, making him feel at home. Others just greeted him, some still ignored him. Do you know who he became friend with? With those who gave him the most attention and dedication, of course! That was what he wanted to receive when he arrived. As a consequence, he was willing to help them when they needed it.

The greatest example in serving was the master Jesus. He came to serve. That's why they loved him so much. He said: "And whosoever will be chief among you, let him be your servant (Matthew 20:27)." In other words, if you want to be served by the world, you must first serve it, then you will reap the rewards of your act. Offer love and love you will receive. Help and you will be helped. Smile and receive a friend. But ignore the next one and he will ignore you. This is true both in personal and professional life.

A wise advice is to treat others as you would like to be treated if you were in a similar situation. If you do that, you will surely be a winner. This is one of the biggest secrets of success. Few know it, so few are successful.

Some time ago I was in a company, giving a lecture and I saw that the employees wore a button, with the design of two eyes and a smiling mouth. A simple design; two black dots and a curve. Below it was written: "SMILE". How beautiful! It really marked me. The smile is indispensable. Wherever you are, whenever you look at someone, do it with joy and a smile on your lips. **A smile captivates anyone.** The smile is also very important on the phone. Speak with joy, but without exaggeration of intonation. The joy in the voice is felt by the person on the other end of the line. Talk to people, as if you are talking to a loved one. Speak with the same joy that you would speak to your loved ones, without using the terms of affection, of course!

Take care of the lamentations! They are a contagious plague. I have two examples. The first is from a couple who only discussed the problems in private. They always expressed joy in front of their children. They were cheerful and usually didn't complain about things. On the contrary; They always tried to improve situations, thus making the home an always pleasant environment. The other example is from a company. All administration from different departments I met, always had the same answer, when I greeted them and asked how they were, they answered: "Tired. I worked hard and tomorrow I will have a lot to do again." On this occasion, some classes were set up for an English course. Everyone came complaining that their minds were tired and they would have difficulties in learning. The result? A total failure! Everyone dropped out before the course ended!

Now, I ask, "Was the company enslaving them"? No! It was not. They worked only eight hours a day. The problem was that the administration did not realize that a vicious circle of lamentations gradually formed. One complained, the other copied, and so on.
The result was that the managers of each department were replaced and the employees were re-educated. Those who did not enter the new climate, which was a joyous one, were fired sometime after the administrative staff had

been. The company changed totally and started producing more and grew up from that time on.

Don't complain! You can't imagine how contagious it is and how quickly it spreads. Observe your country. Maybe you have freedom, home food, public health assistance, etc. But even so, whenever people can, they spend hours talking badly about the government and regretting what they don't have, instead of being grateful for what they have already achieved. I have seen this happen in the United States, Brazil, France and many other countries that may have a much better life than yours.

The next day Dhay met a street vendor who called him by name and offered him a potion, which he called magic. Dhay was startled. How did he know his name? Was he an "Enlightened Being"?

Before Dhay could ask, as if reading his thoughts, he replied:

- I know your name, I know a lot more. I'm a magician.

- Nice! Teach me this trick!

- It's not a trick. I'm not a trick magician. I'm a wizard.

- Wizards don't exist!

- Too bad you don't believe me! It could guide you to the next treasure: "the worker bee".

-Of course, magicians exist!

By the way you look like a great magician.

Dhay joked, as if asking for his help.

- I know everything, I see everything, I am "the wizard!"

- How much does the worker bee cost?

- I don't work for money. But I can't just give it to you. I will show you how to get it. Then you will have to pick it up yourself.

- What should I do?

- You must penetrate the supernatural. To find it you will have to go beyond this life.

- Where?

- Deep within your soul. To catch it you will have to travel beyond your imagination.

- How should I act?

- Just have the desire. If you wish from the bottom of your heart, you will succeed. If not, you can return to Brazil and forget the "Enlightened Being" and the unlimited power.

- Why that?

- **The unlimited power is within you!** Now you will have to dive inside your soul to get this treasure! When you return you will know where to look for the next one. **If you do not accept the challenges you will never win!**

The wizard, then, like magic simply disappeared leaving only a little glass bottle. Dhay took it and realized it was empty. At least that was what it looked like. He picked it up and took it to the hotel.

At the hotel he opened the bottle and started to feel dizzy; everything started to spin and he passed out. When he woke up, he was at the peak of a mountain. From there he could see the neighboring countries. He saw an old building and people crying inside it. They were asking for help. Suddenly, he was no longer in the mountain, but in front of the building. He asked what help they needed and a weak old man replied that they needed pity. At this point a great and bloodthirsty man appeared and demanded them to give him their lives. The old men begged for mercy and the giant demanded their lives to turn them into gold and silver. Only then did Dhay see that the giant's eyes were made of diamonds.

The giant began to slaughter the old men who could do nothing. They only asked for mercy. With each taken life his eyes became brighter and his body bigger. When the giant left, Dhay followed him and arrived at his home; the most luxurious one of the place and it was all in gold, silver and diamonds. The giant then blew the souls of the people he had killed into a cloth bag and took the street again. Dhay forced a window and entered. He opened the bag and the souls flew out, but as soon as they left, they became gold. Dhay understood then that the giant's wealth was made from the harvest of the lives of others. He looked out of the window and saw a city of giants and millions of men, women and children being turned into gold by them. While they were crying, the giants rejoiced and grew more.

Suddenly, Dhay threw up a gold nugget. He picked it up and grew a little. Only then did he realize that the giant had returned. The giant said, "Welcome home." These lives are yours, so that you have the strength and size to dominate others and thus become a powerful giant. Dhay looked at the giant and saw just behind him, above his head, a glass on a shelf with a worker bee inside. He asked why it was trapped. The giant said it was the symbol of honesty and hard work. He said it could not be released or it would destroy him. He said that each of us has the worker bee inside us, as well as the gold nugget. He advised Dhay to keep the bee well attached, otherwise he would never be a giant. He would never have the power to turn people into gold with the bee free.

Dhay then took a golden vase and hurled it against the bottle. It shattered, and the bee flow away. The giant then touched Dhay and he began to turn into gold and the giant started to become smaller. He laughed a lot because, according to him, he would easily trap his bee again. "Giants are hard to destroy"! At that moment Dhay opened his eyes and there he was back at the hotel apartment and no longer saw the bottle with the magic potion. However, he saw a small worker bee flying free out of the window. He immediately understood that his journey to the depths of his soul was over.

Everything was clear to Dhay. He had gotten the message. He was becoming more and more sensitive to interpretations.

The countries he saw represented the world. The old weak building represented the miserable people, the suffering and wronged people. The giant represented the world's powerful men who act unscrupulously in search of profit and power, even destroying people to achieve it, killing by hunger, war and morally.

The souls transformed into gold and silver represented the profit obtained illegally, at the expense of other people.

The fact that the giant's eyes become brighter means that the human being, the more he has, the more he wants to have. His eyes were diamonds. Diamond is wealth, and wealth is what people seek.

The fact that lives flew out of the bag and turn to gold means that unscrupulous people take what they can from the weakest, destroying their lives materially and spiritually; for the miserable cannot have happiness but starving, sadness, cold and watching their children suffer.

The city of the giants represented the dominion of the powerful in the world.

The nugget that Dhay threw up means that we all have a desire to grow within us. The fact that it was vomited means that the power to grow is within us. Therefore, we do not need to enrich illegally. We can get rich by working and using intelligence, without taking what is from others.

The lives that the giant offered Dhay to grow and become stronger means that we can be supported by unjust people and manipulated to do the same. Then he remembered the minister who had proposed that millionaire illicit business.

The worker bee, trapped in the glass, represents the workers who work exhaustively, as slaves for an insignificant salary that do not meet the basic needs of human beings. It couldn't be released because it represents honest work. We are either honest or dishonest, there is no middle ground.

The fact that he broke the glass and freed the bee and then turned to gold means that we have to be careful when acting against more powerful people. Finally, the fact that the giant says it would arrest the bee again, means that even when someone's bad actions are discovered, this someone can do them again in the future.

Now Dhay knew that the worker bee was not a bee, but an exploited and manipulated human being. But then what does it mean to "seek the worker bee"?

Dhay then went to the window to see what was going on outside. There was a man shouting: Co-co-coconut candy, kids, it is a trifle the price of coconut candy."

Dhay remembered that he had seen and heard that guy many times, but he hadn't paid any attention to him. Now he knew; he was a worker bee. Now he understood that to obtain the worker bee meant to work honestly. He had learned a new lesson. Sometimes things are in front of us and we don't see them. Yes. The worker bee represented honest work.

CHAPTER IX

THE GREAT LEADER

Dhay again decided to consult his book. He opened it at random and read: "Never lose sight of your goals. Never forget them."

He thought about it ... What was his goal? He had traveled the world! But what for? To get the unlimited power that was inside him!

Now he understood better. When he got the real dog, he had to donate it right away. The dog was worthless! He had achieved something within himself. The bee was not a bee, but honest work! "EUREKA! Exclaimed Dhay. His eyes opened. The treasures were symbolic. Each treasure he conquered he had acquired a new virtue. He was step by step, getting unlimited power!

Yes! That should be it! Maybe not ... But one thing was sure. It was necessary to seek the treasures and the long road would develop his talents and give him unlimited power.

At that moment the "Enlightened Being" appeared to him and explained the secret of each of the treasures already obtained.

- Hello Dhay!

- Hi, what a surprise!

- I came to bring you a little more light. I will explain to you the meaning of each treasure conquered so far.

- Meaning?

- Yes. Had you supposed that there would be no reason to travel the world in search of treasures?

- Well, everything is very confusing.

- This is because you have not yet learned to see with the spiritual eyes. When you learn, you will know the meaning of life. The first treasure, was the seed that you should plant and let a strong plant grow. It represents patience. To achieve success, you have to wait patiently for many facts to unfold. Success requires years to wait in many cases. By waiting until you found the right seed, planting it and letting it grow, you learned to be patient, because you were not. However, the conquest of treasures represents only the beginning of total conquest. **We must develop our skills day by day throughout our lives**, including patience.

The purebred dog represents humility. To conquer it, you were subjected to very great humiliations, such as the one imposed on you in Brasilia. Today you understand that being humble can bring us great rewards. The dog itself was worthless. It was not necessary to keep it with you. It was only the symbol of the humiliations that you would pass to conquer it.

The valuable diamond represents love, as your mother explained. In the search for a diamond, you had the opportunity to prove your love in many ways and you did.

- What if I hadn't shown my love? Had I been selfish?

- I would appear to you one last time, to inform you that you had failed.

- That would break my heart!

- Sometimes we only learn through pain and the loss of what we seek most.

The seedling of the noblest tree represents purity. You proved your purity by respecting Lyn's doctrine and not trying to make her break her chastity and also not accepting the politician's illicit business. Being pure is something that very few achieve. Many have lost the chance to achieve unlimited power through lack of purity. This is one of the most difficult missions.

The worker bee represents hard work. This attribute you had already achieved in the search for other treasures. The conquest of this only confirmed what was already yours. Laziness is present in 100% of failures.

The "Enlightened Being" then told him to seek the next treasure, (the great leader) and disappeared.

Dhay met a man named Jader on a Sunday afternoon, and it changed his life. They became great friends and he taught him great lessons.

What really came to influence his life was a long conversation they had one night while having dinner at a restaurant.

- Dhay. Have you ever stopped to think who you are?

- Who am I? What do you mean?

- Yes, simply like that, who are you…?

- I'm Dhay, I'm an adventurer, I'm a son of God …

- Right. What else?

- You know... I don't understand what you mean ...

- You are much more important than you think. You have a splendid curriculum. A knowledge that a minimum percentage of men have. You traveled a lot. You learned the secret to success.

- Did I learn? And which one is it? I haven't realized yet!

- This is the point. We don't realize what we have. We seek to acquire power, knowledge, success, money, etc. But we don't realize what we already have. We just look forward. We run after what we don't have yet. We have to think more. We have to find out. We are powerful, but we don't believe in our potential. We let ourselves be overwhelmed by disbelief. Pay close attention because an act or a word can change a man's destiny. And the act of speaking to you now can change your life, Dhay. Pay attention to every word that I will say to you.

- OK.

- **I don't believe in luck. Everything has a reason.** I would like to begin by telling you the story of a boy who once accepted an offer to sell books door to door. He did not have the gift to sell. But always before making a decision, he would say a prayer and think about how he could best act in each situation. Sometimes he was sure of what he wanted but after the prayer he felt that he should act differently. Different he acted. Always, according to his words, following the influxes of the spirit.

One day he went to sell at a school in the city and sold nothing. However, he met a book writer who used to do some extra work there during his free time. One word led to another and the writer found out that that young man had the special gift of communication in addition to a lot of knowledge in the area of motivation. He encouraged him to write a book on the subject. He gave him a card with the phone and promised to help him with the book edition process when it would be finished. Sure enough he discovered that he really liked to write and now lives off the many edited books. Now I ask you. How did it all begin? Accepting a proposal that went against his natural will. He heard the influx of the spirit.

- Do you know anything about logic?

- Much! And do you know something?

- Not much. But I try to run away from it. I believe that **great opportunities arise when we act against logic.**

- It is a two-edged sword. Logic, as the word itself says, represents something logical. Something probably right. Avoiding it, when you feel the burning desire, can lead you to success overnight. Acting against logic requires prior study and a lot of boldness.

A friend of mine, acted against logic and found the opportunity of a lifetime. He was looking for a job and got nothing. He decided to act different from the standards. Then he picked up the phone and called an English school. As He knew that most receptionists do not speak English, which is not the spoken language in his country, he spoke English with her. The receptionist asked him if he did not speak her language. He in English explained to her that he spoke. The secretary, not understanding what he was speaking, called the director. Cool! He was now able to speak to the person who could actually solve his problem. The director asked him to send a resume. Arriving at the school, (instead of sending via e-mail or any other means) he spoke again in English to the receptionist and was automatically taken to the principal. At the office, the director asked him what country he was from. He then confessed not to be a foreigner, and started part two of the plan; now face to face with the director perplexed by his boldness.

Instead of saying that he was there because he needed to work; he said he was there because he knew that the company was looking for a professional with the characteristics he had. He then started to detail what he had to offer to the company and explained how the company would profit from having him inside. The director at the end of his explanation looked at him and said: "Young man, we are not really hiring and I don't know where you got this idea from, but I am perplexed by your boldness. You know I'm a very busy guy. Don't you know that"? That was the question my friend needed to deliver the coup de grace. " I know. That's why I'm here! To enable you to grow and at the same time have someone who can take care of part of your work. We could grow together, because I see no better way to grow than by uniting the brains of determined people to succeed! I can start working immediately!" The headmaster's eyes bulged, he had a tremendous, bold and shamelessness one, before him. Exactly what he needed! Today this guy is general director of companies from all over Latin America. At the time he started, the company was small and had no branches. All it took was just ten years of dedication from the two new co-workers.

This was a beautiful example of how to defy all logic. The logic would be to ask for a job. This was a beautiful example of boldness and determination in the right way, in the right measure!

Boldness and defying all logic are two ingredients that must be used cunningly, wisely, with a previous, deep analysis, in order not to have a negative effect. If applied well it will give good results. The current market is lacking in attitudes that defy all logic. It is also lacking in bold people. For sure the greatest men in history are bold people.

It is very important to be superior to vanity and pride. We have to know how to level ourselves up so that our neighbor can understand us. **We have to have attitudes**

worthy of admiration, towards the president of a corporation, as well as towards the shoeshine boy. For that, we don't need to lose our power to command, nor do we need to hurt our own pride.

The arrogance of many leaders has made them lose the affection of subordinates and once dissatisfied, human beings will use less of their potential. **The arrogance of leaders leads many companies to bankruptcy.** Worst of all, leaders do not even realize that the business sank day after day, because employees didn't do their best due to dissatisfaction.

Empathy, my friend! This is the secret! Empathy! When you can understand what your neighbor is feeling, you will know how to act in order to build him up and when that is done, you will have become his hero. Then he will give you all possible support.

Never forget that the human being we love most is ourselves. When someone demonstrates loving us, admiring us, he ends up winning us over. So is the human being. So are we.

Something very important within this theme is praise. Sincere praise is the most practical way of earning the respect and admiration of others.
If you praise the person to himself, he will be happy. If you praise him to others in front of him, he will be flattered. But if you praise someone to the others without

the person knowing when he knows about it he will be forever grateful and will have extreme admiration and gratitude toward you.

Remembering important dates such as birthdays is something remarkable. Even of people who are not family. You will be remembering one of the most sublime moments in this person's life. If you give the person a gift it will be perfect. But make sure it is something that the person can keep, because every time he sees this souvenir, he will remember you. This may seem silly, but little things like that make a big difference.

Success is like a card game. It doesn't always depend on good cards, but on how we play with the bad cards. People tend to think that being important and known by everybody means to be successful but it may not be. You are successful if you feel like that. **Success is within you. Work to earn it and you will get it.** Anyone who thinks that someone is successful without hard work is mistaken. That does not exist! But we can work hard without getting tired or if tired, even though feeling well, when we like what we are doing. That is why it is important to choose well what we want to do.

- Many, however, are financially successful, because they inherited from their parents ...

- It's true, Dhay, but they will have to work hard to maintain it. Both the name and the capital. Or are you unaware of the many cases of people who threw away everything they inherited?

- Yes, you're absolutely right.

- Dhay, if we don't work hard and do not use our intelligence to maintain what we have we will lose all. Many say, "I want to win the lottery and get rich so I won't have to work anymore." I tell you; these are the ones that when they win if they do, will throw everything away in no time. Then they will find excuses and more excuses for the failure because **it is normal for human beings, not to assume their own faults, but to attribute them to others.**

How many friends lost, how many failed businesses, how many broken homes, just because people chose to blame their actions on others? Take care of yourself Dhay! We do this daily, without realizing it. Remember: **Take your responsibilities, your glories and defeats, as well as your mistakes and work hard on them, then you will be a winner.**

I really like Theodore Roosevelt's example. He became a great writer, but few know that he had extreme difficulty with writing. He said that he used to work like a slave in order to put what he thought on paper. That is, he was no genius, but a very dedicated worker. That's why he became a great writer.

-And luck? Don't you think it exists?

- The luck? As I told you, I don't believe in luck. There is a meeting of opportunities. Those that everyone has in life. Some catch them, others don't. But the opportunities come for everyone. The fact is that some are prepared to embrace them, others are not.

- Can you explain it better?

- Chances appear every moment. For example: Your country's education minister resigns. Why don't you take over?

- Because the President of the Republic does not call me!

- Why not?

- Because I'm not ready. I have no study for that.

- Did you get it? If you had dedicated your time to politics, worked hard, studied with total dedication, etc. You would have that chance!

- I got it.

- What you have decided was not to be a politician! Surely if you look hard for what you want, you will get it! Many people lament the lack of opportunity, but do not realize that it is all about qualification.

One day a friend joined a company and worked hard. He worked hard, showed interest in making the company grow. (This is the point. The more you dedicate yourself, the more recognition you will have and the more success you will have). In addition, he was always at the side of the boss, making himself available and helping him in everything. Not to mention the fact that when he asked for a job, he didn't arrive at the company looking like a poor guy, saying: "I want to fill out a form because I need to work".

He brazenly picked up the phone and told the secretary, who was calling to see if the director was there. (He had previously discovered the director's name and asked for his name, not his title). She logically wanted to know who he was and what he wanted. My friend then said his name and said that the matter was private. She asked him to wait for a moment; (probably, she spoke to the director) and immediately afterwards she announced that he was not available that day. My friend thanked her and said he would call later to make an appointment. He was previously informed that in the afternoon another receptionist would be performing the function. The afternoon arrived he said he was there to talk to the director, and informed the receptionist that he already knew who he was. (He had already spoken to the receptionist in the morning and she had communicated it). The receptionist informed him that unfortunately he was in a meeting and could not see him. He, with the air of an important person, (which he was not) and dressed nicely in a suit and tie said there was no problem and asked the receptionist to make an appointment as soon as possible. It was done! A meeting was scheduled for the end of the afternoon, right after the meeting!

Half an hour before the appointment's time, there he was, reading the newspaper while waiting. The director would have no way of escaping him.
Soon after, the director appeared in the reception area and my friend on the other side of the large room, discreetly, giving the impression he was reading the newspaper, watched the director and the receptionist talk about him. He kept waiting, because he could see them, but not hear them so he didn't know what was going on. The director returned to his office and afterwards the receptionist informed him that he could not talk to him in that moment. It was hard! He then rescheduled the appointment. The next day he was there half an hour early and when the director arrived, he was face to face with the "man". Shamelessly, without giving a damn about the receptionist, he addressed the director and, smiling, greeted him. He, almost without option, invited him to go to the office upstairs. It was better to talk to that boring one soon or he would come back. My colleague then, after describing his entire resume, explained how he could be useful to the company; he never asked for a job. He was hired! He was trustful and showed what he could offer to the company instead of "asking" for a job. In other words, he basically

did the same as the other friend I just described. This technique works!

- Yeah. I already realized that daring is important. I am building my path step by step, with boldness and determination.

- Great! I felt it in you. That's why I'm telling you all these things. I know you will make good use of my words. But for most people it is a waste of time to speak. They will never understand and will never put it into practice.

- I am firmly convinced that it is necessary to know exactly what we want to achieve it. Otherwise, we will be like someone who gets lost in a forest. One day he will find the way out if he survives, but before that he will be in the dark for a long time, only then to reach the goal.

- Yes. Absolutely, Dhay. Now I will tell you a secret that I call "the secret of the gods."

- Wow! What's it?

- This is powerful! Pay attention to your subconscious. It is paramount for everything to conquer.
Have you heard of people who sense what is about to happen?

- Yes, Jader. I even know when a close friend or relative dies before receiving the news.

- Then you'll understand me! Our spirit has the power to feel anything, anywhere. We just have to develop that gift so we can know how to act in the face of a doubtful situation. **"At every moment, particles of thought pass through our brain". (Nésio da Silva). We have to be aware of what is important. Among these thoughts, there are tips from our subconscious, on how to act in relation to the decisions we have to make.**

The problem is that people don't believe that. They do not know that this power exists within us.

Do you put that into practice?

- So-so. Now it's clearer! I will be able to use this power better.

- Dhay, do not discuss this with anyone, unless you are sure that the person will be able to understand you.

- I know. People would think I'm crazy and criticize me a lot. Well, I don't really care who makes destructive criticisms. The world is full of them. I now remember a friend from São Paulo, who lives in Curitiba, Brazil. He was criticized a lot and people, due to their wrong attitudes, told him that he would be nothing in life. He then decided that he would prove the opposite to them. (I actually think he tried to prove it to himself). He started doing his best and today he is an exceptional professional;

Very good in the area of architecture. But I am firmly convinced that we must leave criticism aside and stick to praise, because in the world we live in, it is rare for someone to pay a compliment. If someone praises us it is usually because the person really liked what we said or did.

- Whenever you want something, think about it and think about it daily. Create fantasies, imagine yourself with your goal in your hands and your subconscious will provide a way to materialize your goal. Remember that what you think you attract. This applies to friendships. Fool attracts fool, wise attracts wise.

- I know that, but sometimes it is difficult to do things, because besides, people do not help, they get in the way.

- Certainly. But work hard and do something big, so big names will be by your side. Great people will feel inferior and will be happy to help you and be your friend. Now, I tell you that in order to do something big, the best way is to talk to your subconscious. It's your best friend and literally talks to you. And best of all, your brain always has all the answers. Don't leave it talking to itself, because what it says to you is the "steps to success".

- Really. I will read more about this subject.

- The author "Joseph Murphy", is the best I know on this subject. He has several books on this subject. In fact, we must read many books on the subjects we want to learn. Thus, the subject will be recorded in our subconscious and it will start acting within these principles.

Dhay decided then that he would travel to America. Two days later he was back in Salt Lake City, Utah. Why he came back, he didn't know. He went to the Mormon temple square, where he had received the book that had guided him ever since.

Perhaps the "Great Leader" he was looking for was the president of the United States, but that was not what his heart said.

He sat there, watching the people passing by. It was already getting dark and Dhay looked for a hotel. He was feeling a little lonely. He was missing his friends and his parents.

The day dawned and Dhay admired that beautiful sunrise from the balcony of the hotel room. The sky with a few white clouds and some on the horizon, orange by the rays of the sun. A fascinating sunrise. He woke up very excited and determined to find the leader he was looking for.

He returned to the room and looked at the definition of the word leader in the dictionary: "Person of great evidence". Damn it! That he already knew!

He went out into the street and his heart sped up! There she was. His sweet Lyn.

- Lyn, Lyn! Here, wait. Shouted Dhay.

Lyn turned and saw him running back.

- Why are you here?

- I was in Israel and I decided to come here.

- Tell the truth, Dhay. Why do you travel around the world?

- Lyn, I don't even know. I run after what I don't know.

- An adventurer?

- Perhaps. How about you? Did you move here?

- Yes. Shall we have lunch?

Later, after being introduced to Lyn's family and having lunch at Lyn's home, Dhay and Mr. Robison sat down to talk. Later, Dhay would understand that he was not there by chance, but an important lesson would come from there. The important conversation they had started when Dhay noticed that Mr. Robison had notes taped to the refrigerator door, in the library, in the bathroom and elsewhere in his home.

Mr. Robison explained that certain important things that we have as goals will never be realized simply because we end up forgetting them. Then he puts notes on the wall and they stay there until such a thing had been achieved.

The conversation really got interesting when they started talking about leadership. This was very interesting to Dhay, because he was looking for "the great leader" and had no idea where to find him.

Let me report this conversation in full, as I know it will be very useful to you who are looking for to be a natural leader:

- How to know what is right?

- That's easy. Bow to the creator and ask for inspiration in everything you have doubts. If you do it with faith you will know how to act in each situation.

It is also very important to observe what we are going to say, because also by our words we will be judged.

- It is true! The chance of winning friends is often lost by saying the wrong things. My father always said that the right way to win people's friendship is to show interest in them instead of trying to make them interested in ourselves, since human beings value themselves first and then others.

- For sure.

It is also good to treat everyone as we would like to be treated. It will make them love us. Loving us they will do anything to help us.

- Something I learned in my trips around the world is that a smile captivates any heart. If we always receive the surly people we know with a smile, we will end up winning their respect and friendship especially if we reach out to help them when they need us. But a fake smile doesn't work! It is a great way to show falsehood. That is why we must prepare ourselves daily to feel happy and thus be able to smile with joy and honesty. A Chinese proverb says: **"A man without a smiling face should not open the store"**.

When you smile your voice changes and people realize that you are happy. Smile. It costs nothing! In fact, **our happiness is the size we imagine it in our subconscious.** When people learn to be happy even because small things, good things start happening in their lives! If they forget to appreciate the joyful moments, immediately they feel unhappy. The right way however, is to ignore the bad things that happened and start building happy thoughts again. So said Shakespeare: **"There is nothing either good or bad but thinking makes it so"**.

- It is true! I met a woman full of bitterness. She was never happy. She simply used to refuse to talk about good things. There was always an enemy to criticize. A small mistake of someone and the person would become bad in her perception. Everything good that had happened no longer mattered. In other words, she chose to live with bitterness and sadness.

Whatever you think about day to day you become. Think every day that you are rich, that you are happy, that life smiles on you and that will be.

Let me say something I suppose you don't know! However, answer me first, what word do you like to hear the most?

- I don't know, but I think it is my name.
- Exactly! If you want to make someone feel good, always address people by their names from the day you first meet him/her and forever. Unconsciously this person will like you. We must also not forget to give personalized attention to the client, friend or whomever.

- I met a guy who when someone called to talk to him, his secretary, instructed by him, said he was busy and asked that person to call later, just to look like a highly busy professional. He missed getting many customers because everyone likes to feel unique, not as just one more. He will seek the services of another professional, who can give him attention. If you want to be successful, you must attend to the client immediately, whenever possible and never show anxiety in saying goodbye. In doing so, he will give exclusivity to your establishment, in addition to bringing you many other customers. When facing with substantiated complaints, be receptive and let the person know what action will be taken and take it! The client will not forget the promise you made and will be expecting you to follow through. Also remember, that if you serve him well for many years and at a certain point you fail with him, it will be enough for him to forget all the years of good service and he will abandon you.

- Based on this behavior, I hung a sentence on the wall that says: **"Here, only the best is acceptable".** It is thinking about doing the best, that I always follow some providences. These providences should be followed by any leader, who wants to have the respect of his subordinates, customers and anyone else.

- And what are they?

- First, the appearance. I struggled for many years to be a leader. Do you know why? Not to have a boss telling me to have my hair cut, but when I started to manage a group of people, I found out that I needed to be respected by everyone and I had to have my hair cut because long hair does not change the quality of the person, but most people don't trust long haired people because many of them don't care much about their responsibilities. Maybe in a few years it might even be fashionable. It is not now. We must present ourselves in the standard form of the time in which we live and in accordance with the standards of the position we hold.

Also, it is important to take care with the vocabulary used. We must use it as the language we speak commands. No slang, and bad words.

We should also not procrastinate our affairs, as this will cause problems and our subordinates will understand it allows them to do the same.

The word leader suggests to lead, to guide. How can we lead someone to the north if we go to the east? What we say and what we do must be the same. We must lead by example. That way we will make our subordinates respect us spontaneously and this is the only way to get the most out of them. If they act under pressure, they will only do what is expected of them when they are being observed. Whoever does not have the respect and spontaneous submission of employees is just a boss, not a leader. A leader is the one who manages to influence people and make them follow him because of his examples and acts without forcing them to do so! The true leader is the one who when someone makes mistakes, instead of cursing, teaches him and remembers that the subordinate is a human being, not rubbish! The true leader doesn't let a birthday go by. He praises when there are reasons for doing so and he helps every time that it's necessary to give the example and be closer to the employee. He must be convincing, his orders must be firm, but he must be like a kind father, rebuking sometimes and at the same time showing love. Be the one that subordinates consider a father, a brother, a friend ... Humility is an attribute of God and only the wisest men have it.

I have worked at a television company and aimed at a leadership position. For that, I started to exercise leadership. I helped everyone and wanted to learn every task. Soon I became very handy, within the company and in a short time the board counted on me for many things. The employees, whenever they needed something from the board, preferred to ask me to intercede for them. They knew that if I interceded for them, they would probably be served. However, an employee got close and paid no attention to me. One day I went into his office and told him that I needed him to teach me some tricks of my work so that I could do it better. He gaped, flattered and promptly helped me. I commented on his help with others and he was very happy, because I always helped everyone, but I never needed help from others, but he, yes, he had been asked to help me who never needed help! He became my great friend and we started to help each other.

As soon as everyone respected me as a leader, I took over as manager. The company started to grow quickly, because everyone wanted to be helpful to me, who before taking over management, had helped them so much.

The leader must always know how to assume his own mistakes and also those of the team. That's what he exists for: to lead, to receive the honors and also to be held responsible for the mistakes of the team, which he coordinates. Assume the mistakes! Take on no lies! Without trying to make the mistake or problem smaller than it is. But don't blame yourself for what you shouldn't, this is harmful. Each measure should be aimed at those who really deserve it.

One day I was late for work. My superior wanted to know why. I said I hadn't woken up on time. He replied, "I hope it won't happen again!" When I was leaving, he called me and said, "Thank you for being honest. We need honest leaders." From that day on, he started assigning me more important tasks, because he had discovered that, even in embarrassing situations, I would not lie and I became the person he trusted.

We often fail to progress for lack of goals. But much worse is spending time on meaningless goals. Program yourself and your team! Go out and get it! Be bold! Be determined! Keep laziness away! The market is in need of people with these attributes.

- Everything you told me is very interesting. I also think, that people don't progress by working on things they don't like. Wrong professions.

- You can be sure of that, Dhay. Most people, take the first opportunity that appears regardless of whether they like that profession or not. They will never be able to work with love. They will never be happy and will never give their best. This is perhaps the worst mistake. We must try hard to be able to work with what we like so we will do our job well and be outstanding people. Nor will we lose our temper so easily with subordinates. We will make the profession a pleasure, not a curse in our lives.

- Yes! We will even do small things well done, which are sometimes very important. I remember the story of the American President McKinley: He was once on the bus, (before being president), with a friend. An old lady got on the bus and her friend continued to read the newspaper quietly. As there were no benches left, the old lady stood up. McKinley then stood up and gave her the seat. Years later, already president, McKinley, had a vacant position of trust and was in doubt about this friend and another. He remembered what happened on the bus and gave the job to the other.

- Interesting.

- We talked about honesty earlier. Something that is part of the key to success is found in a sacred book, called, "The Book of Mormon". In this book, a man named Helaman, leader of the people at the time, took the seat of supreme judge and did so in righteousness and equity, striving to keep God's laws and commandments. So, he and the people prospered on earth. (Helaman 3:20). If we act righteously, everyone will trust us and the keys to progress will accumulate over us and we will grow quickly then.

- In my trips I discovered that we can always learn something from others. No matter how simple or ignorant the person is, something can be learned. For sure every person we know is superior to us in something.

- I have no doubt that what you say is true. Therein lies one of the great secrets of success! Be humble to learn even from enemies if possible. However, for people to be willing to transmit something to us, it is necessary to captivate them first.

- Do you know any special techniques?

- Yes! The first step is never to say that the person does not know what he says or does. Say that and there will probably be an enemy at your side. Never discuss a subject with the person if they are closed to dialogue. Never impose your opinion through authority. You will never convince anyone.

- You mean, we always have to agree with others?

- No! We must get the other person to think like us. We can often use a person who can influence them better than we can.

- Can you give an example?

- Yes! One day, working at a small service company, I realized that it would go bankrupt. I needed to do something, but I had no active voice, because the manager, a radical woman, only heard the voice of the women of the company. The fact is, I had the solution to save the company. But if I gave the idea, I would not be heard. Her husband, a great friend of mine, had an active voice with her. I told him my idea and at my request, he suggested it to the manager as his idea. He wrote down the names of many businessmen I knew and passed it on to his wife. The idea was approved and the company got many new clients and rose. He got the glories of the idea, but so what? We both know that we have cunningly built the company. Me with the idea and he with the suggestion.

- Thus, we will not be recognized!

- That was a special case! The goal was not to bring glory, but to keep the company running, thus keeping my job.

One day Lyn was working as a saleswoman for an appliance store and a customer asked for a camcorder. He looked at it and found it expensive. He started citing advantages over the camcorder of the competitor. My daughter patiently listened to him and instead of trying to convince him, she agreed with everything and said that she also thought it a good option to buy the competitor's camera. The customer was amazed. What to argue? There was no way! My daughter agreed with him! Surprised he asked if she would have the audacity to buy the competitor's camera. He wanted to know if she wouldn't lose her job doing that.

At this moment Lyn enters the room:

- I said, no! We had the freedom to buy wherever we want. However, I added that I would buy the brand I was selling, because in addition to having all the advantages of the competitor's one, I had some additional advantages of paramount importance. The customer couldn't help himself and asked what the advantages were!

Great! Now he was receptive! He made a point of listening to me. I sold the camcorder and a few days later he came back with a friend, who insisted on buying from me.

- That's right. Now imagine if Lyn had tried to convince him by disagreeing with him, saying that the other camcorder was not so good. She would lose the sale for sure.

- That's my baby!

- Yours? No! Mine! Said Lyn's father. Everyone laughed.

Another way is to conduct the conversation, in order to get the other person to offer what you would ask for. So, you in the perception of the other, are accepting his idea and there is no resistance.

- For example?

- A father was looking for a job for his son. There was a vacancy in the company where he worked. However, he did not want to ask his boss for the job for his son, because if his son did something wrong, he could compromise him. The suggestion should come from the leader. As if he didn't know about the vacancy, he commented to the manager that his son had decided to stop working at the company he was in. He also said that he would not like his son to leave, as he was a good employee and it would be a shame if he quit his job. Maybe he wouldn't find another so great company. The manager then suggested the vacancy and hired the son without the father having anything to do with the transaction.

Dhay went to the guest room, right after dinner that night. Confused, he decided to open his book. In it he read: "Open the eyes of the subconscious and you will see the light".

He remembered the "Enlightened Being". He called for him. As if by magic, there he was.

- You seek the great leader and you are very close! But take care. Very strong temptations fall on us when we are close to something big.

- More than I ever had?

- You will be hit in the heart. Don't fail, or all your effort will have been in vain.

- Can you tell me about the great leader?

- Yes! That's why I came. Now listen carefully, for instructing the world will be your duty.

I will teach you some steps for successful leadership. When you find someone with these attributes, your bosom shall burn within you. You will then know that you have found the great leader. Listen to him and then go in search of the last treasure, which is the successful human being. To get it I will give you some leadership principles.

Always be honest and if you make a mistake apologize and you will be recognized as great among all. It makes your friends happy and makes them respect you. It also leaves your enemies without arguments. How can they discuss something that you have already admitted to have done wrong? They will end supporting you.

When you give an order, demand fulfillment of the task firmly, but the next moment be smiling and receptive. This will help to maintain friendship with subordinates and at the same time make them follow in your footsteps. Everyone will love and obey you.

Watch out about your intuition. It can fail. Analyze the situation carefully. Observe each point and act without fear, without hesitation. **Show certainty in what you do. This makes others feel confident.**

Listen carefully. Never stop listening to what people have to suggest, as they can often see things you haven't seen.

Whenever there is a disagreement with another leader, listen carefully and analyze the situation. Perhaps you are wrong in the way of thinking, even if everything seems very right to you. **Listening is something that few know how to do. Only true leaders can develop this gift.**

Grumpy boss doesn't work. Take it easy. Show self-control. This will bring you respect and make them love you so they will work for pleasure, not out of obligation. Those who work out of obligation never do it well.

Let subordinates know that you will analyze their opinion. And let them know of your decision about it and they will be encouraged to give you other ideas. Always be available to listen to suggestions.

Always review the pros and cons of any decision, before making it.

- Yeah! There is something that intrigues me. I always analyze the situation well before making a decision and yet sometimes I end up making mistakes. Worst of all, people like to criticize and don't miss a chance to do so.

- Humility! Humility, my dear Dhay. If you made a mistake, accept it is a mistake!

- Sometimes it doesn't work well.

- If you do it the right way, yes, it does! Acknowledging the error, you can imagine the criticism you will receive. Before the person criticizes you, apologize for the mistake. Criticize yourself, but without depreciating yourself. The person will probably come to your defense, justifying that the mistake was not so serious.

Once, a guy, responsible for the company's account, made a mistake in his calculations and was called by the director. Before going to meet him, this young man recalculated and found the error. Arriving at the office before his superior could criticize him, he said: "I have already found out where the error is and I recognize that what I did was unforgivable. Although I dedicated myself to calculating, I was very tired, as it was late at night and I was exhausted. I should never have exceeded the limit of my resistance." The businessman did not criticize him for the mistake, as he had already admitted it. However, knowing that he had worked overtime, he acknowledged his effort and stood up for himself. The aggressor became a defender:

"Okay! Sorry if I was rude on the phone; don't worry, after all"... This was interrupted by the accountant: "Of course I have to worry. Imagine if I made such a mistake with each customer! It would be chaos! Here I have the new calculations! I recalculated as soon as I learned of the error. I hope this can alleviate the damage I have caused."
The businessman then said:
"Imagine! Nobody is perfect. The error was detected before it could cause damage."
This incident served to strengthen the bonds between the two.

- Now it's more clear.

- With regard to convincing people to your way of thinking, never use force. The leader who leads screaming, the husband who screams at his wife to make her submissive, the religious leader who holds the faithful with promises that God will punish those who do not do what he asks, soon they will have no one to lead. Now if you lead with love and attention, everyone will admire you. Never let others dominate you as everyone must demand respect and respect others. It doesn't matter who: boss, employee, husband, wife, everyone.

I'll tell you a story that will show you how to make people defend your idea: "There was a manager at a tourism company, who was responsible for convincing customers who paid part of the installments and ended up discouraged and choosing not to travel anymore, to change their mind. This manager used to set an appointment and asked the person to report in detail the reason for the withdrawal. The client came with the most varied excuses or reasons. The dialogue without much variation was like this:

- Good afternoon! Let me know your problem.

- I changed my mind about my trip to England and I'm here to break the contract.

The manager, whom we will call Paul (a fictitious name), used to say nothing; he just kept looking in the client's eyes, as he felt obliged to add the reasons for the withdrawal. Paul then, used to take a contract termination term out of his briefcase and drop it on the table, just in front of the client. He then would start filling it out and only then did he start talking. At this point, the client who had arrived ready to argue found himself unarmed and was left with no way to argue. Because the manager had already accepted his request to withdraw.

When everything seemed finished, he started to argue. Let me narrate an interview I have watched:

- You are director of the company "The King's Export" and graduated in foreign trade. No! I think I have the wrong contract ...

- No! That's right! It's my contract!

- You negotiate with very qualified people, so ...

- Ah! Yes! With great entrepreneurs!

- Right. So, you are a very enlightened person!

- Thank you!

- Let me see if I understand ...

At this point, Paul puts down his pen and stops filling out the termination form:

- Isn't a cultural trip important for you? Paul asked in a tone of surprise and amazement.

- No! I did not say that!

- Of course you did! You said you are very busy at the moment so it's not important! If it were, you would delegate tasks to subordinates and would not miss such an opportunity to expand your knowledge!

- No! It's not that!

- Ah! good! I was surprised! So, the reason for dropping out is another one...

At this point, all the client's arguments fell apart. Using them would mean being an unenlightened one, with no sense of priorities. Going back on the importance of the exchange was not possible. He would contradict himself. Then he decided to speak the truth.

- Well, actually I decided to go on my own, no longer through the travel agency.

- Ah! Got it. But tell me, what is the reason?

By this time the client was already acting on his own, totally bewildered. Without imagining what the next sentence he would say would be.

- Well, actually I will have more freedom to choose where I go.

- Ah! Got it! You thought it best to give up your cultural trip and opt for a simple leisure trip.

Paul starts filing the termination again.

- Well, since you think it is unimportant to improve culturally, I am sending this request for termination to the finance department so that the due amounts are returned to you, as governed by the contract.

- Boy! You are underestimating me! I know it is important that I improve myself culturally. I'm just going to do it myself, not with your agency, the customer says angrily.

Paul finishes the termination request and stamps it. They just need to sign it. At this point the client would love to have a chance to step back and prove that he cares about the culture. However, he would not humble himself to the point of asking for it.

Paul feels that's the right moment and gives him the chance.

- Well let me clarify one thing, as this is my responsibility within the company. Our program includes the best culturally. You will not waste a single minute with unimportant things.

And the final blow:

- That is why, the most respected entrepreneurs and leaders of this country travel and send their children to study abroad using the services of our company. I think it's unwise for you to give up on this plan, because you'll waste time looking for information and you won't know all the wonderful places that can be visited. If you want we can still keep the contract.

- Yeah ... I was thinking. I didn't quite understand the benefits that I will be receiving. It will certainly be more expensive, but it will be much more profitable.

- That's right!

- You know! You're right! We will keep the contract.

Thus, the customer was maintained. Can you understand that, Dhay?

- Yes! For sure! However, putting it into practice is kind of more difficult. And what caught my attention was that Mr. Paul did not use many words to convince the customer. He simply let him speak and caught him in his own arguments.

- Right! Congratulations! This is the point. Those who talk a lot just "spill the beans". So, open the guard for the other side to attack. Talking a lot is the great defect of most people and sincerely, how annoying to have to put up with a chatterbox!

- For sure!

- Another important thing is to know how to analyze the point of view of others. Understanding why the person thinks that way, but this is a difficult task.

- Right! Then we will know better how to act.

- Exactly. One day a citizen was looking for a house to rent. There was only one problem! He had stopped paying a debt and had his name on the credit protection system, but he was honest and paid the bill as soon as he could; as soon as he overcame the momentary financial difficulty. The fact is that he could not rent a property because the real estate consulted the register and seeing that he was a debtor, did not rent it. He found out who owned the house that he was interested in and went to talk to the owner. Before, however, he analyzed the reasons why the owner would not rent to him if it weren't through the real estate agency. He concluded that it was for fear of not receiving the rent, of having his property damaged and having to bear the expenses. He visited the owner and told him who he was, where he worked, etc. Then he showed him some reference letters with contact phones. He explained that he understood the reasons why he would not rent the property directly to him, but he explained, however, that he did not intend to go through all the bureaucracy of the real estate company, not to mention the fact that as he was new in the city, he had no guarantor and also would not like having to pay fees due to real estate. All of this explained in a humble way, accompanied by letters of reference, made it possible to rent the property without having the credit consulted. But something important was that all the arguments used were real. He didn't lie. He knew that lying would bring him problems, earlier or later.

- But say one thing, "Enlightened Being"! Does it all work so well in practice?

- Yes! It seems unrealistic but the human mind is very predictable. The most successful people are the ones who know how to deal with it and let me warn you. Do not use this power for evil. Never use it to harm people, because there is a law that rules the universe. It is the "boomerang" law, everything we do comes back multiplied for us.

- Can you give an example?

- Yes! If you help the people you live with, when you need it you will have help. Otherwise, when you need them, they will not help you. If you make illicit profits, one day you will be discovered and you will be liquidated. If you work honestly one day you will achieve success.

- Guy! You are a genius!

- No! I'm not! I am an "Enlightened Being" as you use to name me.

- Why have you never stopped to talk before? You used to give the message and disappear...

- You were not prepared. You used to ask silly questions.

- Gosh! Better I shut up!

- No! What you were going to ask is a wise question.

- How do you know that? I haven't even asked yet ...

- I read your mind. Human beings are predictable.

- How do you do that?

- People's eyes are the doors to the brain. The answer to the question you were going to ask is, "no". You don't have to die to get unlimited power. Just master your mind and you will have all the power. If you totally dominate your mind, you will do everything you can imagine!

Dhay who was standing fell down sitting.

- You read thoughts! How can I dominate my mind 100%?

- Wrong question!

- Excuse me! Do not go!

- I won't! I will visit you frequently from now on. You will soon master the secrets of the mind.

- I won't even question.

- No! You won't, because you are too wise to waste time.

- Teach me more!

- When someone treats you with disrespect, don't fight back. Remember that people have reasons for doing so, even though they have no right to vent anger on others. Try to understand it. Treat everyone with sympathy and respect. They will eventually calm down, apologize and start admiring you. Doing so will earn you a strong ally, a great friend. If you return the insults, you will win an enemy. Jesus Christ said it well: "You must love your enemies".

- To compete with others... does it mean not to love them?

- It depends what competing means to you. Trying to be better than the next one is extremely healthy. It is a stimulus to improve. This helps you to overcome limits. However, trying to disturb others so that they are worse than you is acting in an unproductive way. You will become a loser and still hinder the growth of others.

- Everything I'm learning is so good! But sometimes I am afraid to face everyday situations. Traveling the world in search of treasures has been a test of fire.

- This is natural for human beings! I'll teach you a little secret. Whenever you have a difficult situation to resolve, don't delay. The situation is always easier than it seems! Lift your head and face it!

I remember that one day, I had to mow the lawn in the garden. I didn't do it for a month. It looked like a forest. My wife, tired of waiting, asked her friends for help. I was ashamed! Two weeks later, I got my act together, took the mower and mowed the lawn. It was easy! At times even fun. I suffered much less than the mental suffering I had procrastinating. I had thought every day: "I will have to mow the lawn; I will have to mow the lawn." That was killing me.

Death is an ingenious enemy, it usually takes us in a second and most of the time the person doesn't even suffer, but it torments us all our lives. It never fails to return to our thinking. So is fear. Psychologically tortures us and only leaves us when we face the situation imposed on us.

- And when leading ... How should we rebuke a person so that he accepts the rebuke with good cheer?

- Teach in the form of a tip. For example: "I have to congratulate you on the friendly way you treat our customers. This certainly yields many others. Keep it up ... I'm very happy with your way of working. I will give you a tip so that you can captivate them even more. Always keep the binder in alphabetical order and all the cards saved after use. That way customers will admire you, not only for your friendliness, but also for your organization.

- Fine! Thank you for the advice.

- Oh, come on! You do not have to thank me! It is my duty to help you in whatever way possible. After all you are so dedicated! You deserve!"

In this way the secretary's morale was raised and at the same time the work that was being done poorly was charged. The secretary is sure to do her duty with pleasure in order to feel useful and be praised more often.

- How can we identify possible leaders in the team?

- To identify a potential leader, look at who colleagues are looking for when they need help. There is the born leader. Being a leader is within us. It is born with us. If you want to know who will be the leader in the future, look at the children's groups and you will see that there is always one that is respected and their opinions are respected. Usually there is only one leader in a group, as they are still children, they do not know how to act as a team and one tries to be stronger than the other. One of the two ends up leaving the group. This happens even among animals. There is always a leader in the group. If a stronger animal arrives, it dethrones the other and starts to lead the group.

- In a company, this is negative. Isn't it?

- Yes. Leaders must live in harmony and help each other so everyone grows. If the company is doing well, salaries can be increased, branches opened, and new leadership positions are made available. That is why we must always work to generate new leaders.

There are two types of leaders: those who lead, but do not form new leaders, and those who lead and know how to improve employees to become leaders.

This second type is exceptional, as soon there will be other leaders leading other subordinates who will be at your disposal. Thus, the company acquires structure to grow.

Many companies go bankrupt because they lack these elements in different departments and so the company grows and reaches a point where control is lost and then starts the bankrupting process!

The true leader always listens before speaking. But those who speak before and often do not even let others speak are false leaders. They won't get very far. Higher positions will not be available to them. For the results they will obtain will not justify their rise.

I like leaders who set an example of work and are motivators. But those who only rule are not true leaders.

- But shouldn't they delegate the work?

- Yes! For sure! But that doesn't mean to be lazy. There are tasks that are too important to delegate to any

subordinate but you should certainly delegate everything possible. Thus, the subordinate will have the chance to improve and become a leader. John F. Kennedy rightly said, "Don't ask what your country can do for you. Ask what you can do for your country."
- He was a great sage.

- I like to be called a dreamer. To hear my children and wife say to me: "Stop dreaming! Put your feet on the ground!"

The true Leader, first dreams, then seeks ways to make the dream come true. The loser seeks people and only then, lulled by the dreams of others, does he dream of the crumbs of others' dreams. Go in the shadow of others, if he does not find a true leader who will dream for and help him to seek it, he will never accomplish anything.

- I am fascinated by the determination and ability to dream as well as the faith to fulfill the dream of a man named Adolph Hittler. Too bad he used his power for evil. He could have been as big as Ghandi and even more.

- Yes, Dhay. Dreaming is the principle of fulfillment. We have passions in life and dream of achieving so we struggle and achieve realization.

- Rightly said Nésio da Silva: "Our passions make us what we are".

- My heart barely restrained when I heard Marcos Groth's dreams. One day I asked him what his professional dream was and he replied: "Having the largest language teaching network school in Latin America". Wow! Today there is a single school in Curitiba, Capital of Paraná, Brazil. I have my doubts whether he will reach beyond his dream. Determined man he is! I'm sure he can do it! But let me tell you; he is helpful, intelligent and hardworking."

At that moment Mr. Robinson slams the door and the "Enlightened Being" disappeared.

- Dhay, why are you in Salt Lake?

- I do not know! I am looking for a great leader and I felt I should come here. Is there a great and wise leader here?

- It depends what kind of leader you are looking for ...

- I don't know ... I seek the wisest of all!

- The wisest is in heaven! However, there is a representative here on earth! I assure you that he is the biggest and wisest in the world today. However, few know him. In him the hand of God rests! This man is a prophet of God!

- A Prophet!? Alive? But ... No ... Well ... I mean ...

- Dhay! Listen! I don't know why you're looking for a leader. But if you are looking for a great leader, this is the greatest of all.

- Where can I find him?

- In the sacred Temple! He's my friend and I can introduce him to you.

The next day Dhay was introduced to the prophet and his heart was overjoyed! The peace he felt was indescribable. His words never left his mind. He had been transformed. He no longer felt like a mere mortal. He now knew the value of love. He knew he was infinitely small compared to the creator, but he also knew that he could become like him one day, after death. He had finally found the penultimate treasure. Only one was missing.

EPILOGUE

The successful human being

Dhay knew ... Now he was close to the goal. He wept with emotion! It only remained to look for the "successful human being". The last treasure! He planned to propose to Lyn!

- The "Enlightened Being" appeared to him! Lying in the guest bed at Lyn's house, he was startled by the sudden appearance of the "Enlightened Being", who spoke to him!

- Dhay! Pay attention! You're close to the goal! Soon you will have the power you seek! You're much closer than you think! But something you have to do will break your heart.

- Ok... Can I know what that is?

- To reach unlimited power you will have to forget Lyn. You cannot have that knowledge if your heart is given to a simple mortal.

- ...

- There are inferior things and superior things.

There was a hermit who lived in a cave. He only went out at night. On one occasion he tried to go out during the day, but his eyes accustomed to the darkness met directly with the bright sun and he almost went blind. Since then, he has never tried to go out during the day again. He had been born in the darkness of the cave and so he chose to die. One day, however, a lone rider passed by and dropped a box of matches. The hermit after months found use for the different sticks he had found. Every day he burned one. He wished he could see the details of the cave hitherto hidden. One day he accidentally set fire to the straw on his bed. The entire cave was lit up. He applauded standing. He put sticks, twigs, logs! He didn't let the fire go out! The light of a single stick no longer satisfied him. His eyes now accustomed to the faint light of the fire, he endured the light of a cloudy day outside the cave and when the sun appeared shy among the clouds his eyes already accustomed to the partial clarity endured that new portion of light. His dark days were over!

- What does that mean?

- It means that the human being is accommodated. He gets conditioned to something and doesn't want to give up what he has until he finds out that eating mango is better than eating lemon. One day he discovers that a feast is better than mango and mango is no longer satisfying. You have overcome many trials and today you have all the knowledge you need! We just need to go out into the light!

- How do I get out into the light?

- First, go back to Brazil. Alone!

- Can I stay another week?

- You can. However, remember that the peach, once ripe, will rot in just a day or two! Don't cry over mistakes. There are irremediable things, like death. Once it happens, nothing more can be done.

- When would it be wise for me to leave?

- Tomorrow afternoon! You are about to see the sunlight!

Francisco Beltrão, Brazil.

Dhay took a few days to rest. A month later, he went to the theater, "O Espaço da Arte", in the same one where years before he had attended Edgar Farinon's lecture, but there was a big difference. Now the speaker would be him, three days from now and entitled to the handshake of the mayor of the city and other leaders. Dhay was a little confused. His father had scheduled the lecture without telling him. He trusted his son and was in the habit of "pushing" his commitments. Dhay ended up meeting his father's expectations.

- Nervous, Dhay?

- No, Dad ... I'm extremely calm. I love your surprises, said Dhay. I don't even know what to say at the lecture!

- I suggest talking about what you've learned. Not about what you saw!

- Why is that, Father?

- Because today you are a wise man, some two days were enough to realize that! I'm very proud of you! I scheduled the lecture so you will be able to help a lot of people in this city.

- Public speaking scares me, I never spoke to many people at the same time.

- Remember that not even the mayor knows even half of what you know. You are like a teacher in a literacy class. I remember one day when I was called to speak at the church. I prepared the topic and was shaking as I went up to the pulpit before starting the speech, I looked into the eyes of some of the audience and realized then that they were ordinary people, in large numbers, but ordinary. I spoke and left the pulpit. At the end of the meeting several leaders came to congratulate me on having approached the subject in such depth.

- You're right. For someone who traveled the world, what is it to say a few words to a hundred people from the countryside!

- That's it my son!

Espaço da Arte Theater.

- It's an honor to be here today. I have known so many cultures and many wise men. I learned many things, but something important was to understand that **living the situation is the best way to understand the point of view of others.** I mean that if we want to know what it's like to feel the pain of spraining a finger, just sprain one. There is no other way. Nor can we know the taste of a fruit just by explanation. We have to prove it. This taught me to put into practice an indigenous saying: "Never judge your brother, without having walked a few miles in his moccasins".

I also saw a lot of suffering and loss of opportunity because of procrastination. We must act now. **Postponing**

prevents people from developing their full potential. Benjamin Franklin said: "Don't put off until tomorrow what you can do today"!

Go ahead! Do it right now! However, **remember that in everything we do we must seek perfection. We must produce masterpieces!** We must always criticize ourselves in order to improve, as well as being susceptible to criticism from others. I am not saying accepting all, but analyzing what they say and having the courage to admit to being wrong and to change when wrong. But be careful when criticizing. It can be fatal to a friendship or your career. I quote another sentence by Benjamin Franklin: "Speak ill of no man, but speak all the good you know of everybody!"

I am very concerned about the way we act, because time passes and never comes back. It is unfortunate, to spend time on trivial things. Only fools like to do it. Spend your time on useful things! I like English writer **Dr. Samuel Johnson's phrase; "The habit of looking on the bright side of every event is worth more than a thousand pounds a year."**

Remember, you who are oppressed and discouraged; it is never late to restart! Never make the mistake of spending your precious time, playing, drinking, watching TV, etc. These things are for leisure time, not to fill the whole day. In a world that has existed for millions of years, we live less than a century! Therefore, live your life intensely!

Many are the ones I saw, giving up when facing the failure. Each failure brings us closer to success because to fail we have to make mistakes and each mistake serves as a learning experience so every time we make mistakes, we learn something that we must do differently next time. Learn to persist and get up whenever you fall. Learn to glimpse the good things, because the human being tends to see everything that exists in a bad sense! We tend to remember what we lack and forget to enjoy what we have already achieved.

I can't stand grumpy and complaining people, who complain about everything. Who think to have nothing. If you are that type, I ask you: Would you sell your eyes or legs to get everything you want in life? No!? You mean your wonderful little body is worth more than anything in this life? What do you complain about then? Don't you feel ashamed? I saw many complain about having to wear slippers; I particularly like it a lot. What then you tell me about the one-legged ones? Wouldn't they give everything to be able to walk barefoot? Guy! You're a winner! Just being born makes you a winner! How many millions of sperms have ended their life by the time you hit the egg? At that moment, we literally won a race against millions! Are you able to try to win millions here today? No? Are you unable to overcome your own discouragement? Then you're a loser! Get up, put yourself free of your fears, go to the battle and win again!

It is time to learn how to value ourselves and to value others. A person who feels valued is able to overcome the highest obstacles! Sincere praise softens even a heart of stone!

Dale Carnegie in his book "How to Make Friends and Influence People," tells the story of a pesky boy named Tommy. He was a problem at school. The new teacher in the class, Ms. Hopkins solved the problem. She began by praising the students for their achievements. She said: "Rose, beautiful dress the one you are wearing! Aline, I heard that you draw very well! Tommy, I heard that you are an exceptional leader, I will need you to make this the best class of the year!" She then began to praise him for all the good he did, letting him know that she thought he was a good student and he did not disappoint her.

Dale's wise advice is that we should give someone else a good reputation so that they feel interested in maintaining it.

As well as praising and making the other person feel useful, it helps them do their best; criticizing negatively destroys self-esteem. Call someone incapable and they are likely to feel and act like that. Except for a few who will do everything to prove otherwise. These have great chances of winning.

The speaker Edgar Farinon once said that he had worked in a company and that there was an employee who produced little. He would probably be fired. He started talking to him day after day and found that he did not feel able to do the job for which he was assigned. That's because his leader criticized him every time, he didn't like the results. Edgar started commenting on all the good things he observed in the way he did the work and suggested changes in the flawed points, always remembering that he did it because he felt that he had an exceptional potential to be developed. After being praised and given advice day after day, the employee started to feel competent and see that in fact his superior complained about everything and everyone; he was a failure as a leader! He then became one of the best employees in the company and soon became a leader. Soon he was superior to his former leader.

Do you know why? Because he believed he could! Because when he was praised, he realized that he had the capacity to perform the functions to which he was called.

Another effective leadership tactic is to be friendly, cordial and honest. Subordinates to be effective have to love and trust the leader.

Above all, be like the father, mother, friend of the subordinate and the subordinate will spare no effort to carry out effectively the function assigned to him. When you have to reprimand your subordinate, do it, but not in a rude tone. Do it with determination, but without showing anger. Point out the error and then the way forward to avoid making any more mistakes. If necessary to repeat the explanation, do so with pleasure. Remember that the employee is not your slave, but someone who sells you the services. Treat him as you want to be treated, after all the employee is nothing without the boss and the boss nothing without the employee.

In the area of finance, never forget that big savings are made by saving on small things. As an example, the telephone, water, electricity, shoes, etc.

However, remunerate your employees in the best way you can, as a well-paid employee has a strong incentive to work harder. However, if earning well is stimulating, earning little is highly demotivating. Do not expect to have good employees, for a long time if you pay them poorly. An idle employee must get what he deserves, as well as the worker. **Each human being is given according to his value.** A good way to do this in addition to salary is giving monthly performance bonuses. This will pay more to those who deserve it and encourage everyone to have better results.

A great way to give orders is to ask and not to order. Something like: "John, can you please …?". This makes the employee happy because he is being treated as a friend and not just as a simple employee.

When possible, gather your team for a moment of leisure, on behalf of the company. This makes employees like the leader and also the company, but always without exaggeration, thus not making it impossible for them to spend part of their time with the family. An ideal time is when they reach the company's monthly goals. Everyone celebrates together and feels motivated to hit goals again in the following months.

Avoid harassing an employee in front of a client or coworkers. This is humiliating and shames him. It creates a feeling of contempt for the person of the leader and a feeling of dissatisfaction with the company. With these feelings an employee will never give the maximum in his service.

Exalt the employee in front of others, whenever he deserves it and he will do his best to respond to the compliments and get them back.

Not everyone here is an entrepreneur and that's why I speak to you now as a citizen of society.

I start by reminding you that there is always someone watching us. Listening to what we say and seeing what we do. **Our actions and words can influence an entire society. Our words and actions are worth taking as a good example.** When you're talking to someone, be constructive,
always praise what you have to praise and refrain from criticizing others. If a friend of yours criticizes someone, just listen and if you know the criticized person, mention two good things you see about him. If the criticisms

extend, discreetly, change the subject. If that doesn't work out, it's better to sneak out.

Always show a happy face. Look in the mirror and you will see the best posture. A happy face helps to captivate people and consequently make friends and close deals.

Never get into an argument to force another person to think like you. You will not achieve it this way. State your point of view only once and don't discuss it unless the person is open to dialogue. Getting into discussion is a perfect way to make enemies.

Avoid being a nuisance to others by being present on occasions to which you have not been invited, or staying beyond the time allotted on occasions when you have been invited. Finally, use common sense.

Always show optimism and be optimistic, even in difficult situations. Do not complain about the problems, but instead find positive points in the disappointments. Never bow your head. Be the master of the situation. Don't let yourself be overwhelmed. People who manage to do this way are the ones who excel over others and are successful in life.

Finally, I would like to remind you that nothing falls in your lap.

Nobody gets rich overnight. Nobody is suddenly admired. Everything is built step by step. Great friends are acquired through small gestures, day after day. Great wealth is achieved with excellence in work, day after day. Those who think that they will conquer the world with dishonesty are wrong. Dishonest work is the face of failure. For once discredited, there's no more chance to the citizen.

Many have asked me what success is. I always answer that success can be begging on the street or owning the greatest wealth in the world. It may still be to get married and have a bunch of children or live single and independent. Success can be achieved in any situation. It depends on the point of view of each one. **Success is success only if we consider it so.** There is no point in being considered national heroes if we feel like failures. Success is within you. Do what pleases you and you will be a successful person. Success exists only in people's minds. That is why I tell you if you are unhappy with what you do, you are a failure. Change it now! **Find out what is pleasing to you and do it and you will have found the secret to success, because it is within you!** As well as unlimited power is in you.

The dream is the embryo of fulfillment. So, dream! Be proud to be called a dreamer. Dream and then roll up your sleeves and work hard to make your dream come true. Dream, because **the world is only what it is because citizens like you and I dared to dream!** Dream and ignore pessimists; the losers who ridicule you because you believe in a dream, because you believe in an ideal. By not being able, they try to make you as miserable as themselves. Dream, because dreaming is a unique attribute of the winners!

Dhay came home happy. He had given a lecture to hundreds of people and received very strong applause. In the end, celebrities shook hands with him in thanks for the lecture he taught.

At night when he was preparing to sleep, the "Enlightened Being" appeared to him.

- Congratulations! You got all the treasures! I'm proud of you!

- No! The last one is missing! The successful human being.

- Didn't you find him?

- No ... did I? I do not remember...

- Dhay ... How do you feel?

- Wow! Accomplished! I spoke at the lecture about success! My life is a success for me!

- Good ... tell me ... Regarding the last treasure ... where could it be? Who could it be?

Dhay thought for only 2 or 3 seconds. His eyes lit up.

- I am the successful being! I became one, day after day! I am the last treasure! Is it right?

- Sure it is! Congratulations! Now is the time to use your knowledge for the benefit of others. Our knowledge is worthless if it is not shared.

Unlimited power is within you, just develop it. Everything we think with conviction if accompanied by action, becomes reality. Be it good or bad. The human mind is the most powerful thing on the whole material and spiritual plan. We just need to learn how to use it. Mentalize something and be convinced that it will happen and work for it and it will be so.

- Live principles of full righteousness. Seek greater knowledge of the spiritual laws that govern our universe.

You can now go out into the world teaching others to acquire the knowledge you have gained.

Be aware that you have been chosen to transform people's lives and make them better. Teach everyone who is thirsty for knowledge each of the treasures you have acquired. Here you have overcome the first phase of your development. We will now begin to develop your mental power in order to obtain things that the world considers supernatural, you will now develop the power of your subconscious.

Dhay then decided that while he was being taught in this second phase, he would go around the world teaching through lectures. From that day forward, he would do everything to make this world a better place to live. He would try to turn this world into a little piece of heaven for everyone who was willing to learn from him. He understood now that he had entered in search of triumph, a search that would last his entire life.

From that moment on, each day of his life would be dedicated to perfecting the use of each of the treasures found and he was sure that he was ready to win many other treasures and each one of them would be passed on to anyone who showed interest in growing. He had been visited by the "Enlightened Being" and now more than desire, he had the responsibility to dedicate his days to teaching all who were engaged in Search of Triumph.

THE END

Every end contains a new beginning in itself.

Soon in bookstores, new adventures of Dhay in "The Unlimited Power of the Subconscious."

Points to ponder

Chapter I

- No one can grow without knowledge.
- Specialization is one of the secrets of professional success.
- Knowing your own business deeply is essential.
- No matter where we are, we can make progress, just knowing the right way.
- We must be attentive to make the right choices in life.
- Things are simple, but man does not believe in simple things and always finds a way to complicate them, thus moving away from the path of prosperity.
- Another secret to success is we must work hard.
- Each chance is unique, don't miss it.
- Not everything we decide to look for at a certain moment, is the best for us.

Chapter II

- Everything that will happen, good or bad, in our lives depends exclusively on the actions of the present.
- Everything that comes to us serves to make progress.
- A single action can change a lifetime.
- Spend as many minutes as needed talking about other matters as per customer satisfaction.
- We should always radiate joy, this is one of the great secrets to captivate people.
- The greatest sage is the one who listens and is humble to learn from others' experiences.

Chapter III

- Everything can be done when you want.
- Listen to everything and speak only what is necessary and what you feel is useful.
- Once respect is earned, we can lose it by a single action or word.
- The true leader never loses his temper.

Chapter IV

- Patience is the attribute of the gods.
- Impatience and pessimism kill human beings spiritually. Keeping calm keeps us resistant, because nervousness wears us down spiritually and physically.
- We must abandon old foolish habits and traditions. Analyze everything and see what makes sense. We must also love others as we love ourselves. This will be good for everyone and bring us many friends.

Chapter V

- Focus on your goal. Forget everything that won't help you get to it.
- Never worry about the distance you have to go, just focus on the next step. Remember the wise popular saying: "look after the pennies and the pounds will look after themselves!".
- Always keep the goal in mind. How to achieve it, God will show you, if you believe.

- Spend only on useful things. Always invest in what will give you a return.

- "If you want to get rich, save what you earn. Any fool can win. But it is necessary to be wise to save and use wisely." (Brigham Young).
- Some become rich because they dream and make plans and are never too lazy to fight and are never happy with what they have. They always seek more.
- Never judge a book by its cover.
- Work always seems more tiring than it really is.
- Procrastination disturbs us day after day, year after year.
- Most of the time things are not what they seem!
- Take care of old habits. They limit growth.
- We should always work on something we like. The work is too exhausting when done unwillingly!
- The absence of a defined goal is the main enemy of success.
- The biggest and most important things go unnoticed in the eyes of men, because they find them insignificant.
- If you want to win, focus on the tasks you have to do and forget the unimportant things.
- A Book on the shelf serves as much as a fur coat in the summer.
- Don't waste time, because it doesn't come back. Each second once passed is gone. What is not done in this second may never be done again and if it is, you will have to use the time that would be used for something else.
- Dream is the first step towards achievement.

- Just dreaming is not enough. We have to plan every step towards realization and work without laziness and without fear.
- If we believe that we will win and work hard for it, it will be so.
- Never fail to make friends. The more you have the better. The more chances you will have of receiving support to carry out an enterprise.
- Try to find out what the person likes and talk about that topic.
- Listening is very valuable, because in addition to making people appreciate us, we also have a chance to learn, because while we speak, we are not learning, but while listening we learn.
- "There are two things to aim for in life: first, to get what you want; and, after that, to enjoy it. Only the wisest of mankind achieve the second" (Borghild Dahl).
- Look back and remember your worst days and then you will see how much you have to enjoy.
- "Never say, I'm destroyed, never put limitations on your thoughts, never be too lazy to try to accomplish something that seems impossible to you. Work hard to make things come true. Remember that you can get what you want. Believe in it and work hard for it.
- Everyone has feelings like you, so treat them as you would like to be treated.

Chapter VI

- Opportunities pass "in the blink of an eye", not to mention the fact that they usually come in camouflage.
- The past is gone, the future does not exist, the present is real and tangible, so do what you have to do, now.
- Many goals are simply overlooked because they have not received due attention.
- Something that brings us down is the fear that sometimes disguises itself as shyness. If we do not face difficult situations and obstacles, we will get nowhere.
- If we knew how to use 100% of our mental capacity, we would be similar to God.
- Based on this principle, if you believe that you are capable of making your dream come true, you will!
- A frank and enlightening conversation can often change a man's destiny.
- Don't lie to your customers.
- Never lose sight of the objective.
- Sometimes we get worried about trivial things, unimportant details and we end up moving away from the goal or when things start to get difficult, we simply choose something easier, thus moving away from our goals. Hence the great number of frustrated people who work in services that they hate, but never have the courage to seek what they dream.
- To seek a professional dream, the way is to study! Study hard about what we want for ourselves!

- The company will only work well when the boss and the employee work in harmony.
- It is necessary to be able to talk on an equal basis with people from different social and professional levels.
- Try to match the best, try to be even better than the best and then this world will be one of prosperity.
- There is not a single human being who has not already failed on the path of success. Failures happen, but we must not let ourselves be overwhelmed by them.
- Don't be ashamed to move on after a failure. It is shameful to bow. The pain of defeat is better than the shame of never having tried.
- The human being, most of the time seeks to hide the error, accusing the closest ones.
- Criticism turns friends into enemies.
- A sincere compliment softens even a heart of stone.
- Never give up. Remember that discouragement brings down almost everyone. Those who win in life are those who overcome discouragement, who persevere.
- Patience is one of the divine attributes.
- Be good, reach out and this will yield you a multitude of friends and benefits.
- Sympathy will make you love the others for their kind of being and that will gain you, their friendship.
- You are only superior or inferior professionally, but as human beings, as children of God, we are all the same.
- Value the next one, because you can find him when climbing, as well as descending on the ladder of life.

Chapter VII

- We should always put recreational activities in our day to day. This eliminates fatigue.
- It is also important to have a view of the consequences of what we are going to do. For sometimes it is not profitable to carry out what we have in mind. We must always measure the pros and cons.
- Adapt to different situations. Act in a way that pleases people, but do not let yourself be dominated and act with sympathy and calm or with rigidity and authority, as the occasion requires, but never be exalted. If necessary to impose your authority, do so without losing control.
- If your employees are not efficient, train or replace them, otherwise your enterprise will sink.
- The employee must act immediately and perfectly and never postpone what must be done immediately.
- Do not deviate from your goals. Always keep them alive in your soul. Nothing should stop you.

- People are afraid of dreaming. (Rudimar Olkoski).
- All successful human beings accumulate defeats in their careers. But they know how to lift their heads and start again. They know how to envision the final victory and use their own defeats as experiences. They become strong and reach the top they dreamed of.

- Things sometimes seem simple, but they can be much more complex than they show. So, all the diligence can be little. We should never underestimate anything or anyone.
- If something is to be yours, no one can take it from you except yourself.
- "Smaller than my dream, I can't be!" (Lindolph Bell.)
- Much of our talent is wasted for lack of audacity.
- Mood is the driving force that takes us to the top.
- "No one can achieve success for you". (Jo Couder). - Success is being able to do what you like the way you like it.
- Just look to the side and you will know how much we are blessed.
- We have to focus on the right things and make them the basis for fixing the wrong ones.
: "We always think about what we don't have, but never about what we have. This is the great misfortune in the world". (Schopenhauer).
- Only good readers can acquire enough knowledge to become great. Through reading we can share the great truths told by the greatest geniuses who passed over the earth and perfect this knowledge by making us wise as well.
- There are two goals in the life of human beings! The first is to get what we want and the second is to enjoy what we got. Only the wisest people enjoy what they have achieved" (Borghild Dahl).
- Persistent effort is the point between success and failure.

Chapter VIII

- Jesus said unto him, If thou canst believe, all things are possible to him that believeth. (Mark 9:23).
- "We need to have a deep and dynamic desire to learn." (Dale Carnegie).
- "It is a thousand times better to be silent than to criticize". (John Wanamaker).
- "Do not speak bad things of anyone and say everything good that you know of each person". (Benjamin Franklin)
- If you don't have anything good to say, stay quiet!

- Criticism is present in 100% of broken marriages.

- when we want something, we have to show the advantages that the other person will have by helping us.
- A smile captivates anyone.
- The unlimited power is within you.
- If you do not accept the challenges, you will never win.

Chapter IX

- We must develop our skills day by day throughout our lives.
- I don't believe in luck. Everything has a reason.
- Great opportunities arise when we act against logic.
- We have to have attitudes worthy of admiration, towards the president of a corporation, as well as towards the shoeshine boy.
- The arrogance of leaders leads many companies to bankruptcy.
- Success is like a card game. It doesn't always depend on good cards, but on how we play with the bad cards.
- Success is within you. Work to earn it and you will get it.
- Take your responsibilities, your glories and defeats, as well as your mistakes and work hard on them, then you will be a winner.
- It is normal for human beings, not to assume their own faults, but to attribute them to others.
- "At every moment, particles of thought pass through our brain". (Nésio da Silva).
- We have to be aware of what is important. Among these thoughts, there are tips from our subconscious, on how to act in relation to the decisions we have to make.
- Chinese proverb says: "A man without a smiling face should not open the store".

- Our happiness is the size we imagine it in our subconscious.
- "There is nothing either good or bad but thinking makes it so". (Shakespeare.)
- Only the best is acceptable.
- Always be honest and if you make a mistake apologize and you will be recognized as great among all.
- When you give an order, demand fulfillment of the task firmly, but the next moment be smiling and receptive.
- Show certainty in what you do. This makes others feel confident.
- Listening is something that few know how to do. Only true leaders can develop this gift.
- Always review the pros and cons of any decision, before making it.

Epilogue

- Living the situation is the best way to understand the point of view of others.
- Postponing prevents people from developing their full potential.
- In everything we do we must seek perfection. We must produce masterpieces!

- "The habit of looking on the bright side of every event is worth more than a thousand pounds a year." (Dr. Samuel Johnson.)
- We should give someone else a good reputation so that they feel interested in maintaining it.
- Each human being is given according to his value.
- Our actions and words can influence an entire society. Our words and actions are worth taking as a good example.
- Success is success only if we consider it so.
- Find out what is pleasing to you and do it and you will have found the secret to success, because it is within you!
- The dream is the embryo of fulfillment.
- The world is only what it is because citizens like you and I dared to dream!
- Unlimited power is within you, just develop it. Everything we think with conviction if accompanied by action, becomes reality. Be it good or bad. The human mind is the most powerful thing on the whole material and spiritual plan. We just need to learn how to use it. Mentalize something and be convinced that it will happen and work for it and it will be so.

Bibliography

The quotations made throughout the book were described at the time they were cited and were based as previously described.

Book of Mormon
 Doctrine and Covenants
 The Bible
Brigham Young
St. Jerome
Joe Couder
Dale Carnegie
Borghild Dahl
 Lindolph Bell
 Rudimar Olkosk
John Wanamaker
Benjamin Franklin
Joseph Murphy
Samuel Johnson
Schopenhauer
Shakespeare
Nésio da Silva
Loreci Ribeiro Farinon

www.ingramcontent.com/pod-product-compliance
Lightning Source LLC
Chambersburg PA
CBHW052311220526
45472CB00001B/72